FRANCISCAN SPIRITUALITY FOR THE 21ST CENTURY

Selected Reflections from the Dating God Blog and Other Essays

VOLUME ONE

Daniel P. Horan, OFM

KOINONIA PRESS

An Imprint of DatingGod.org Productions

Published by Koinonia Press
An Imprint of DatingGod.org Productions

First Printing January 2013

    Koinonia Press
    Boston, MA
    USA

Cover Image: St. Francis; Photo by Daniel P. Horan, OFM
Cover Design: Koinonia Press

ISBN: 061559753X
ISBN-13: 978-0615597539

Horan, Daniel P. (1983 –)
    Franciscan Spirituality for the 21st Century: Selected Reflections from the Dating God Blog / Daniel P. Horan, OFM
        p.   cm.
    1. Spirituality. 2. Franciscan. 3. Prayer. 4. Culture. 5. Politics.
I. Title

12 11 10 9 8 7 6 5 4 3 2 1

To
The Students, Faculty, Staff, and fellow Alumni
of St. Bonaventure University

TABLE OF CONTENTS

ACKNOWLEDGEMENTS

As always, there are many people deserving of thanks. The list is always too lengthy and unwieldy to guarantee that I will not overlook someone who has been supportive, informative, or challenging in my spiritual and theological outlook. But I will offer a small, if incomplete, list here

Thanks, always, to my family – my parents, Kevin and Ann Marie Horan; my brothers, Sean, Matt, and Ryan – for their love and support. I am also grateful to my Franciscan family for the ongoing support and fraternity they offer me in all my work and ministry. I know it is not always easy to understand the complexities of ministry in the digital age but, for the most part, my fellow friars have been largely encouraging in terms of my attempt to navigate this new digital world.

I am grateful for a wonderful group of friends that also love and support me. These friends are legion, but include: David Golemboski and Brianna Copley, Julianne Wallace, Andrew and Sarah Kneller, Susan Abraham, Jessica Coblentz, and so many others. I have had the privilege of getting to know wonderful people as I continue my doctoral studies at Boston College. To my classmates and colleagues, faculty, and staff, I offer my thanks for the supportive and challenging conversations.

Finally, this book wouldn't exist if it weren't for the thousands of readers of *DatingGod.org* who, day-after-day, return to my blog to read, reflect, and share comments. Thank you for your enthusiasm and support – may this book help continue to bring to life what began online.

This book is dedicated to my fellow St. Bonaventure University "Bonnies," those students – past, present, and future. May the spirit of the Franciscan tradition always inspire you!

INTRODUCTION

I never wanted to write a blog.

That *DatingGod.org* even exists is the result of the strong encouragement (read: practical insistence) from the publisher of my first book: St. Anthony Messenger Press, now called Franciscan Media. Lisa Biedenbach, my then-editor, explained to me that, in this digital age, publishing houses wanted all of their authors to have an "online presence." After much hemming and hawing, I eventually surrendered to this request and began writing reflections at *DatingGod.org* on a nearly daily basis.

While I was not the most excited about this project in the beginning, I came to appreciate the impact an author can have and the connections that could be formed by offering reflections of various sorts on a regular basis. The blog became a connecting point between me and a wide audience. I found that I began to enjoy being a part of this online faith community. I made connections with all sorts of people: fellow bloggers, other authors, women and men of all ages and faiths, people committed to social justice concerns, and so many others. I also discovered, rather quickly, that there were plenty of people eager to read my online writing only to criticize my views and reflections. Such is the shadow side of our digital age.

At the time I'm writing this preface I have published 840 reflections to the *DatingGod.org* blog. On one hand, it is an astounding number, representing lots of time and energy. On the other hand, the process itself has shown itself to be life-giving and energizing in its own way (not that it is *always* easy, sometimes it isn't). Whatever one might think of the new digital media that have made self-expression and broad communication accessible to nearly anybody with internet access, I have found this process of "blogging" a helpful way to engage with new audiences, explore current events, reflect on scripture, and "do theology" in an accessible and practical way.

What is presented in the following pages is just a small selection of reflections from the *DatingGod.org* blog over the last two years. I never imagined that the blog would become as popular as it has, with many thousand weekly viewers and hundreds of followers on allied social-media platforms like Facebook and Twitter. It seemed evident that there was a demand for something akin to a "best of" the blog, but I hesitate to suggest that these reflections are better than anything, let alone the best of the more-than eight-hundred reflections published on *DatingGod.org* to date. They are simply a selection of the many entries, each of which is organized into a few categories of thematic similarity. It is the first of what will likely be an ongoing series of print editions of various reflections from the site.

I hope that this book serves as a source of entertainment, inspiration, and reflection. May the Lord grant you Peace and All Good!

Daniel P. Horan, OFM

PART 1

CONTEMPORARY THEMES
IN FRANCISCAN SPIRITUALITY

The (Real) Prayer of St. Francis

St. Francis of Assisi wrote many prayers and reflections on God, but he did not write what has come to be known as "The Prayer of St. Francis" (*Lord, make me an instrument of your peace...*). It is a very recent text. It does not date back to the thirteenth century, but it does represent much of the Franciscan tradition — peace, forgiveness, mercy, and so on. While it is a great prayer, one that Francis would likely not have been upset to have attributed to him, I find a prayer that he did actually write to be something to which I continually return. I want to share that prayer with you today.

Most High, glorious God, Enlighten the darkness of my heart and give me true faith, certain hope and perfect charity, sense and knowledge, Lord, that I may carry out Your holy and true command. AMEN.

March 11, 2011

Francis of Assisi and a Prayer of Importance

These last few days, weeks really, have been rather busy because of the intensive course in interreligious dialogue that I've been co-teaching at St. Bonaventure University. As the program wraps up today and I return to my summer ministry at St. Francis of Assisi Parish on Long Beach Island, NJ, I hope to be able to post reflections and commentary here on the blog more regularly — so stay tuned!

In the meantime, I thought I might share a portion of Francis of Assisi's prayer imbedded in his *Regula non bullata*, the so-called "Earlier Rule" of 1221 that was the long-developed plan of life Francis and his early brothers composed to guide the friars in how to live the Gospel. It is a rather lengthy chapter, offering a unique glimpse into the prayerful heart of the *poverello*, the little poor man from Assisi. He proposes the prayer as a model for the brothers in their daily meditation.

This portion of the prayer, organized as verse 9 in the modern English translation, strongly emphasizes the importance of desiring God above all else, while also highlighting God's graciousness, generosity and Trinitarian presence in the world. Francis is known in his writings and prayers to use lots of adjectives to describe God and God's relationship to humanity and all of creation — this prayer is no different. May his words become ours today.

> Therefore, let us desire nothing else, let us want nothing else, let nothing else please us and cause us delight except our Creator, Redeemer and Savior, the only true God, Who is the fullness of good, all good, every good, the true and supreme good, Who alone is good, merciful, gentle, delightful, and sweet, Who alone is holy, just, true, holy, and upright, Who alone is kind, innocent, clean, from Whom, through Whom and in Whom is all pardon, all grace, all glory of all penitents and just ones, of all the blessed rejoicing together in heaven. Amen.

July 10, 2012

3

St. Francis's Model of Service = Solidarity

Like all Christians, St. Francis didn't begin his life as a Saint. Such exemplary holiness only comes with time as one becomes more and more engaged in living the Gospel life, the *Vita Evangelica*. While it is fair to say that Francis wasn't such a bad person prior to the beginning of his conversion (*pace* Thomas of Celano), we can look back at his life and see in his story a process of ongoing conversion that leads him from a life of average worldly living to a way of being-in-the-world that was centered on Gospel solidarity.

Some people like to associate "service" with the life of Francis, which on one level is innocuous and fine. Yet, there is a sense in which the term service does not capture the depth and complexity of Francis's lifestyle and worldview. Service is something done from the outside, an action or event that occurs in a given space and time. Solidarity, however, is a position or place in the world. It is a disposition or attitude that shapes and informs the way one lives.

Francis was about solidarity with the poor and marginalized, yet not to the exclusion of the wealthy and noble. Instead, his solidarity with the outcast in the world and his willingness to engage the powerful challenged the wealthy and powerful in a prophetic way.

Gustavo Gutiérrez, largely considered the "Father" of Liberation Theology, explains that poverty within the Christian tradition is generally understood in two ways. There is "material poverty," that is poverty understood in the first sense, and "spiritual poverty," a term that has been both helpful and problematic over the course of Christian history.

Material poverty needs little introduction. It is simply the absence of those basic resources that human flourishing requires. Spiritual poverty, a concept that has been used to diminish the demand of certain biblical pericopes on the wealthy and those who minister to the economically comfortable, is rather nuanced and unclear.

Gutiérrez is concerned with exploring a third understanding of poverty, one that I would suggest aligns itself well with the Franciscan understanding of that evangelical virtue. This third approach is that of intentional poverty as both a form of solidarity and protest. Gutiérrez, drawing on God's own example of kenotic impoverishment through the Incarnation, explains:

> Poverty is an act of love and liberation. It has a redemptive value. If the ultimate cause of human exploitation and alienation is selfishness, the deepest reason for voluntary poverty is love of neighbor. Christian poverty has meaning only as a commitment of solidarity with the poor, with those who suffer

misery and injustice.

The commitment is to witness to the evil that has resulted from sin and is a breach of communion. It is not a question of idealizing poverty, but rather of taking it on as it is – an evil – to protest against it and to struggle to abolish it. As Paul Ricouer says, you cannot really be with the poor unless you are struggling against poverty.

Because of this solidarity – which one must manifest in specific action, a style of life, a break with one's social class – one can also help the poor and exploited to become aware of their exploitation and seek liberation from it.

As Gutiérrez notes well, solidarity is a comprehensive and integrated stance in the world. Unlike service work or charity (as popularly conceived), solidarity requires "specific action, a style of life, a break with one's social class."

It is perhaps unreasonable to expect young adults and others today to so radically adopt a position of solidarity in short order, but it is not beyond their capacity to begin to re-imagine what a morally just and particularly Christian life might look like, and then work in ways to make that commitment an ever-more concrete reality. These features of solidarity highlighted by Gutiérrez resound in the life experience of Francis of Assisi.

Francis slowly came to live a life of solidarity with the poor and marginalized much in line with the progressive sequence described by Gutiérrez. At first Francis engaged in a concrete, specific action. The Saint's first official biographer, Thomas of Celano, recounts that Francis was at first "changed in mind but not in body" and apparently took his time appropriating the will of God in place of his own, yet he desired to do so even in the earliest stages of his ongoing conversion.

It was then through the selling of his father's cloth for money to be used in restoring the church of San Damiano that he began to engage in specific actions. He sought to live at the church, without accumulating wealth associated with income, selling all he could to give to the poor. It was in this transition of lifestyle that Francis exhibited the second characteristic of solidarity Gutiérrez notes.

Finally, that famous scene depicting Francis's renouncement of his father and the stability, status and inheritance associated with him, before the bishop marks the definite break with the Saint's social class. No longer was Francis somewhere in the realm of the merchant class and majores of Assisi, but instead intentionally moved to the place of the *minores* or lesser ones who were often outcast or dismissed.

In essence, whether intentional or not, Francis's movement from a place of power, wealth and security to a social location of vulnerability and minority reflected the kenotic character of God becoming human in the Incarnation. It was a self-emptying that made possible the condition for solidarity as opposed to service from another social, economic, and cultural place.

In solidarity one does not fall prey to the self-gratifying condescension that is rewarded in the "giving" of service to another from a remote location. Instead, solidarity depends on the poverty of Gospel life, modeled by Christ and echoed in Francis, that finds its source in the divestment of one's selfishness and self-centeredness expressed in the disassociation with others.

To speak of "Franciscan service" is, in some sense, redundant or at least perplexingly obvious. It should go without saying that those steeped in the Franciscan way of living in this world in the form and manner of the Holy Gospel would be present and attentive to the needs of their brothers and sisters in a way reflecting service as it is popularly conceived. However, the action without reflection on the deeper call to conversion as a movement toward solidarity with those being served is to fall short of the Franciscan contribution to Christian living.

March 5, 2011

4

St. Francis of Assisi and Social Justice

While reflecting on one of St. Francis's *Admonitions* this morning — the *Admonitions* are a series of homily-like reflections the saint delivered to his brother friars as he traveled to different local communities — I realized the relevance his words have for us today. They bear a certain sense of what we've come to call Catholic social teaching, reflections as they are of the Beatitudes of the Gospel. This particular admonition, *Admonition* XVIII, speaks to those who might find themselves siding with others interested only in their own temporal and financial affairs. Like Martin Luther King Jr., who, as we read in my brother friar Steve DeWitt's reflection the other day, is often remembered for his civil rights work but forgotten for his nonviolence and anti-poverty work, St. Francis is often remembered as the peacemaker who "loves animals and creation," without consideration for the radical example and preaching he offered the Church when it comes to matters like private property, money economies, solidarity with the poor, and living the Gospel in a serious, not just nominal, way. Let us reflect on this admonition today, realizing especially in light of the event in Washington, DC, tomorrow,* that the dignity of the human person means more than one issue (more reflections to come on that tomorrow) — and it includes social support for others.

> Blessed is the person who supports his neighbor in his weakness as he would want to be supported were he in a similar situation.

> Blessed is the servant who returns every good to the Lord God because whoever holds onto something for himself hides the money of his Lord (Mt 25:18) God within himself, and what he thinks he has will be taken away from him (Lk 8:18) [*Admonition* XVIII]

---

* The Annual "march for life" anti-abortion protest.

May we be open to the work of the Spirit in our lives to work for a more-equitable society and world in which we do not value our own self-interest at the expense of others.

January 22, 2012

5

St. Francis, Humility, and Preaching by our Deeds

There is a popular phrase frequently attributed to St. Francis of Assisi: "Peach at all times; and, if necessary, use words." I cannot tell you how many times I've seen it printed on bumper stickers, framed posters, prayer cards, and the like. Yet, according to in that particular iteration, you will simply not find that Francis wrote those words. Nevertheless, I believe Francis might find that phrase rather favorable, and his authentic written corpus includes what was likely the foundation for that popular slogan.

In Chapter XVII of the *Regula Non Bullata* (popularly called "the earlier rule" or "the rule of 1221"), Francis wrote: "Let all the brothers, however, preach by their deeds" (v. 3). The setting is the chapter on preaching and who is and who is not granted the faculties – the permission – to preach. Francis understood that good preaching required both natural skill and theological education. Not all good speakers were theologically sound and, likewise, not all the theologically trained are good speakers. Still, all the brothers were to "preach," were to edify and instruct the people of God, in *whatever* it was that they did, thereby "preaching" at all times.

This is really important. This section of Chapter XVII, which provides the initial theme for the whole part of the *Rule*, is actually only a small portion of the section. The remainder, some fifteen verses (the part on preaching *per se* is only 4-verses-long), is all about humility.

What is curious, to me at least, and rather challenging about this section, is that the humility Francis calls for doesn't refer to the typical contexts out of which such a challenge naturally arises. One might think of the need to be humble in

7

situations of leadership or authority, perhaps one must be humble in the so-called secular realm, not setting one's self above another. Yet, these fifteen verses have a lot to do with being humble while ministering.

I get the impression sometimes that people engaged in some form of public ministry feel that they, by virtue of their lifestyle or work, are somehow exempt from the virtue of humility. How often do we cross paths with arrogant pastors, clerical priests, "holier-than-thou" volunteers and the like? What Francis goes to great lengths to highlight is that it is especially those in settings of ecclesiastical and pastoral work that must recall that they should not even own those "successes" or "rewards," but that all things belong to God.

> In the love that is God, therefore, I beg all my brothers – those who preach, pray, or work, cleric or lay – to strive to humble themselves in everything, not to boast or delight in themselves or inwardly exalt themselves because of the good words and deeds or, for that matter, because of any Good that God sometimes says or works in and through them, in keeping with what the Lord says: "do not rejoice because the spirits are subject to you" (XVII:4-6).

Notice how Francis includes even *prayer* as something for which someone should strive to be humble in practicing. I find this passage particularly challenging because, as it is directed at all the brothers, he is reminding us not to focus on ourselves – pat ourselves on the back – when we are doing good *ministry*. It seems so counterintuitive: shouldn't we be proud and self-satisfied when we are doing "God's work?"

Francis tells us: no, not really.

"We may know with certainty that nothing belongs to us except our vices and sins" (v. 7), is the Saint's reply. For those of us who are good preachers, good teachers, good writers, good confessors, good liturgical celebrants, good counselors, good cooks, good tailors, good *whatevers* – all good things come from and return to God. We cannot allow even the good work God does through us to tempt us into thinking it's about *us* individually.

I know that this sort of exhortation is indeed a

challenging one. It can be easy to see how one's ministerial work – preaching, teaching, etc. – can quickly fall into an exclusive camp, undetected by our usual "pride radar" and instead become an object of our own self-aggrandizing. Francis's particular use of the phrase, not to "inwardly exalt in themselves," is especially striking. Pride is not always what is seen or expressed on the outside.

If we do anything that is good in our work, it indeed comes from God. That is all. That is tough to remember. St. Francis, *ora pro nobis.*

July 5, 2011

6

Francis and the Incarnation: Remembering the Importance of Christmas

The other day, in a discussion about the season of Christmas in our local community, a brother friar, who happens to be a well-known Franciscan scholar, recalled one of his favorite stories about St. Francis. It comes from the collection of stories and recollections of Francis by "those who were with him," as the authors refer to themselves, called *The Assisi Compilation.* This particular story is a remembrance of when, on one Christmas, Francis was concerned about taking care of animals, and not just humans. He looked to the poor larks and the need they had to be fed. So he exhorted the leaders of his age, wherever he was, to look after the birds as well as the poor among the human family.

The story actually begins with the Saint's death and how this friar remembered larks coming to the place of Francis's death in order to sing out of praise and thanks for the life of the Poverello. During this reflection, the author moves from the concrete instance of Francis's care for creation to consider more deeply the underlying theological reason for Francis's way of living in the world and why Christmas was so important to him.

This reflection offers us a sound reminder of the

centrality of the Incarnation in Franciscan theology and spirituality. No one, including Francis of Assisi himself, would ever suggest that emphasis on Holy Week and Easter should be diminished, but it is fair to say that — for many Christians — what happens on Good Friday is viewed as the pinnacle of salvation, with Easter Sunday (denoting the Resurrection) as the capstone.

Easter is indeed the capstone, the completion of the Paschal Mystery — the life, death and resurrection of the Lord. Yet, *too much emphasis* has been placed on the Passion in many Christian circles to the overshadowing or exclusion of the Feast of the Incarnation, without which there would be no Easter. For Francis, as it would be for the great medieval Franciscan theologians (here I especially look to my pal, Blessed John Duns Scotus and his magnificent contribution to the theology of supralapsarian Christology), the Incarnation must be given its central emphasis because it was through the uniting of the Created and Divine that Salvation (all of Creation returning back to God) is made possible.

The *Assisi Compilation* conveys this theological focus:

> For blessed Francis held the Nativity of the Lord in greater reverence than any other of the Lord's solemnities. For although the Lord may have accomplished our salvation in his other solemnities [i.e., Holy Week and Easter], nevertheless, *once He was born to us*, as blessed Francis would say, *it was certain that we would be saved*. On that day he wanted every Christian to rejoice in the Lord and, for love of Him who gave Himself to us, wished everyone to be cheerfully generous not only to the poor but also to the animals and birds (AC 14, *emphasis added*).

The reality of God-becoming-human and entering into creation in a particular, unique way gets overshadowed by both the increased commercialism of the civic holiday in the West, especially in the United States, as well as by a popular spirituality that recalls a Mel Gibson-like obsession with the Passion of the Lord. As far as the latter is concerned, an over-emphasis on the last days of the Lord's life reduces the significance of what was accomplished in the birth of God as one like us; truly our brother.

Francis of Assisi helps us to remember that Christmas is more than a day for gifts or a religious holiday to be subordinated to Good Friday, but is in fact the central mystery of our whole faith — God so loved the world that God became one like us and entered into a human-to-human relationship. As Francis said, of course we would be saved!

September 16, 2011

7

Following Francis of Assisi Today: Who Are Our Lepers?

This is the 785th anniversary of the death of St. Francis of Assisi. He is beloved by so many people the world over, Christians and non-Christians, believers and non-believers all admire the man who sought simply to follow in the footprints of Jesus Christ, living out his baptismal promise as one committed to living the Holy Gospel. From popes of his day and the Muslim Sultan Malik al-Kamil, to the last communist leader of the USSR, Mikhail Gorbachev (who, although maintained his atheism, knelt in silence in front of St. Francis's tomb in Assisi for more than 30 minutes in 2008), and the philosopher Albert Camus, Francis of Assisi has captured the attention of billions of people. He was a man of peace, but an ordinary man who, in striving to live as closely to the Gospel way as possible, became an extraordinary example of Christian living in our world.

There is so much that can be said and done to commemorate this saint from Assisi, but I think it's worth reflecting on some of his own story and narrative of the emergence and meaning of the religious communities that call him founder. In an important collection of remembrances of the earliest friars called *The Assisi Compilation*, we read a selection that brings us back to the central charism and character of this way of life.

From the beginning of his conversion blessed

Francis, with God's help, like a wise man, established himself and his house, that is, the religion, upon a firm rock, the greatest humility and poverty of the Son of God, calling it the religion of "Lesser Brothers."

On the greatest humility: thus at the beginning of the religion, after the brothers grew in number, he wanted the brothers to stay in hospitals of lepers to serve them. At that time when nobles and commoners came to the religion, they were told, among other things, that they had to serve the lepers and stay in their houses.

On the greatest poverty: as stated in the *Rule*, let the brothers remain as strangers and pilgrims in the houses in which they stay. Let them not seek to have anything under heaven, except holy poverty, by which, in this world, they are nourished by the Lord with bodily food and virtue, and, in the next, will attain a heavenly inheritance.

He established himself on the greatest poverty and humility, because, although he was a great prelate in the church of God, he wanted and chose to be lowly not only in the church of God, but also among his brothers.

I think that these two constitutive elements of the Franciscan life — humility and poverty — are really important aspects of the Christian life upon which we all can reflect today. That Francis desired the brothers all serve the lepers signifies that they were to transcend the boundaries of social and class distinctions, to risk meeting the stranger and the unknown, to "get dirty" in the messiness of human living, and bring peace, understanding, and love all the while. The lepers were the voiceless, the marginalized, the ignored, despised, and forgotten. Who are our lepers today? Who are the ones that the rest of the Church, society and world wishes to push off outside of our everyday experience so that we never have to encounter them?

They are out there and we are called to be among them.

The humility that Francis sought to instill in his brother friars as he struggled to live it himself reflects the very condition of Christian discipleship that provides the possibility of solidarity and ministry among all sorts of people. A life centered on humility means that one does not consider him or herself above, better, or distinct from others — the rich and poor, the powerful and weak alike. Instead, freedom comes with the letting go of one's own interest, ambitions and goals, the desire for power and dominance, in order to approach all people recognizing who it is they really are: our brothers and sisters.

Following Francis of Assisi today means striving to live among the lepers of our own time in a spirit of evangelical poverty and humility, allowing nothing to get in the way of embracing others.

Who are our lepers? How will we, following the example of Francis, be their brothers and sisters?

May God bless you today through the intercession of our Holy Father Saint Francis of Assisi!

October 4, 2011

8

800th Anniversary of St. Clare's Entrance into Franciscan Life

This weekend marks the 800th anniversary of St. Clare of Assisi's entrance into religious life, having joined the early group of penitents founded by Francis of Assisi on Palm Sunday 1212. To prepare ourselves for this celebration, let us take some time to look at *The Legend of St. Clare* (1255) in which we read of Clare's decision to follow Francis's way of life.

> The Solemnity of the Day of Palms was at hand when the young girl went with a fervent heart to the man of God, asking [him] about her conversion and how it should be carried out. The father Francis told

her that on the day of the feast, she should go, dressed and adorned, together with the crowd of people, to [receive] a palm, and, on the following night, leaving the camp she should turn her worldly joy into mourning the Lord's passion.

Therefore, when Sunday came, the young girl, thoroughly radiant with festive splendor among the crowd of women, entered the Church with the others. Then something occurred that was a fitting omen: as the others were going [to receive] the palms, while Clare remained immobile in her place out of shyness, the Bishop, coming down the steps, came to her and placed a palm in her hands. On that night, preparing to obey the command of the Saint, she embarked upon her long desired flight with a virtuous companion. Since she was not content to leave by way of the usual door, marveling at her strength, she broke open with her own hands that other door that is customarily blocked by wood and stone.

And so she ran to Saint Mary of the Portiuncula, leaving behind her home, city, and relatives. There the brothers, who were observing sacred vigils before the little altar of God, receiving the virgin Clare with torches. There, immediately after rejecting the filth of Babylon, she gave the world "a bill of divorce." There, her hair shorn by the hands of the brothers, she put aside every kind of her fine dress...

After she received the insignia of holy penance before the altar of the blessed Virgin and, as if before the throne of this Virgin, the humble servant was married to Christ, Saint Francis immediately led her to the church of San Paolo to remain there until the Most High would provide another place (Lcl IV:7-8).

Granted, the hagiographical account is a little "hyped" for dramatic effect, but what began eight-hundred-years ago in the tiny medieval town of Assisi — the flight of a young noble woman from her family and comfortable life to follow the

evangelical model of life demonstrated by Francis of Assisi —
changed the course of history for centuries to come.

I imagine she had no idea what she was in for, she had no
idea what would become of her life, but she was open to the
Spirit's prompting in her heart and she followed that call into
living in this world in a way that was most fit for her. May we
discern that voice of God deep in our hearts that calls each of
us to live as we were intended by God to live. We might not
know what that looks like or where it will lead us, but if we are
open to the guidance of the Holy Spirit and strive to follow in
the footprints of Christ as Clare of Assisi did centuries ago, we
might be surprised by where we go and how our lives will be
changed.

March 30, 2012

9

Relationship with God According to St. Clare

When it comes to identifying the sources of Franciscan
spirituality most people begin with St. Francis of Assisi,
naturally. Yet, it is important to remember that although the
poverello was the instrument of God, we might say, through
whom the Franciscan Order was founded, there are many
wisdom figures in the tradition that offer us insight into what
love of God and relationship with God is all about.

We see relational images of the connection between God
and humanity in the writings and example of St. Francis, but
in the writings of St. Clare we see an even-more deeply
intimate expression of what that relationship looks like. In this
passage from her third letter to Agnes of Prague, also a 'Poor
Clare' nun, we read that, unlike those earthly relationships
with lovers that end in deceit and pain, the love God offers us
in relationship is unconditional.

There is a creational dimension to Clare's reflection on
the love of God and our invitation to enter into that
relationship with God even more intimately. She illustrates her
mystical understanding of God's gratuitous outpouring of

God's own self for us through the images of the sun and moon marveling at such love. Ultimately, as the Gospel according to John expresses early in the first chapter, the expression of God's love is most concretely expressed (literally, "revealed" or "disclosed") in the person of Jesus Christ.

Want to know how much God loves you or what the love of God looks like? Look at Jesus Christ, look at his words and deeds and see.

> Place your mind before the mirror of eternity! Place your soul in the brilliance of glory! Place your heart in the figure of the divine substance and, through contemplation, transform your entire being into the image of the Godhead itself, so that you too may feel what friends feel in tasting the hidden sweetness that, from the beginning, God Himself has reserved for His lovers.

> And, after all who ensnare their blind lovers in a deceitful and turbulent world have been completely passed over, may you totally love Him Who gave Himself totally for your love, At Whose beauty the sun and the moon marvel, Whose rewards and their uniqueness and grandeur have no limits;

> I am speaking of Him, the Son of the Most High. (3rd Letter of Clare to Agnes)

January 26, 2011

10

Saint Bernardine of Siena: A Personal Reflection

Saints, like all people, are complex figures. Their personal histories, transmitted as they are by popular and traditional hagiography, are oftentimes presented in simplistic or formulaic ways. This is perfectly understandable because in presenting a canonized saint to the Christian faithful the

Church wishes to highlight those aspects of Gospel life that this or that person exemplified. Yet, there usually remains more to the picture than initially meets the eye, much of which is good and some of it understandably left behind.

Such is the case with the St. Bernardine of Siena (Bernardino Albizzrschi), the fifteenth-century Franciscan saint and namesake of our own Siena College near Albany, NY. Bernardine's life (1380-1444) is one of exemplary sanctity and commitment to the Christian faith and Order of Friars Minor, but it is also a life very much shaped by its historical context. Perhaps best known in Holy Name Province (NY) for his strong devotion to the "Holy Name of Jesus," his popular preaching is what made him famous during his own lifetime.

Cynthia Polecritti, in her doctoral dissertation *Preaching Peace in Renaissance Italy: San Bernardino of Siena and His Audience* (UC Berkeley, 1988), notes that the texts of Bernardine's sermons "are acknowledged masterpieces of colloquial Italian." He was an elegant and captivating preacher. His use of popular imagery and creative language drew large crowds to hear his reflections. And, as Polecritti also notes, the subject matter of his sermons reveal much about the contemporary context of Fifteenth-Century Italy.

A Complicated History

We get a glimpse into the historical context of Bernardine's world when we look at three of the most popular, albeit seemingly scandalous, subjects of his sermons: witchcraft, sodomy, and Judaism. Franco Mormando, author of *The Preacher's Demons: Bernardino of Siena and the Social Underworld of Early Renaissance Italy* (University of Chicago Press, 1999), has dedicated a book-length study to these themes in the Franciscan Saint's preaching. I think it's important to name these topics because they represent two aspects of the history of pastoral ministry worth considering.

The first aspect to recall is that we are products of our time. Today, the things that Bernardine said about Jews or "sodomites" (as Mormando explains well in his book – see Chapter Three – the concept of sexual orientation did not exist in Bernardine's time. He spoke only in terms of "acts," both in the case of males and females) would likely strike the contemporary hearer as abhorrent. His sermons were riddled with ostensible anti-Semitism and homophobia. Yet, the second aspect to keep in mind is that he was responding to the issues of his age based on the pastoral and theological knowledge available to him. Though we, several centuries later, look back and see the concerns of his audiences, the subjects of his sermons and the tenor of the text to be terribly regrettable, Bernardine was motivated by a love for God's people and a desire to address the needs of the Body of Christ in the 1400s.

Mormando sets Bernardine's ministerial stage well: "The world of 1427 was a confusing, frightening place: as Bernardino and his audience firmly believed, the Devil was omnipresent and frequently had the upper hand; humankind was still largely at the mercy of the mysterious and capricious forces of mother nature, and, to add insult to injury, death by famine, plague, war marauders, unjust lords, or absurd accident threatened to carry one off at any given moment." Bernardine's preaching, amid the darkness and fear of the age, brought forth hope and light in the form of Gospel life in an explicitly Franciscan tenor.

Bernardine was well versed in his own Franciscan heritage. One might say that he was a true son of St. Francis, committed as he was to the Observant branch of the Franciscan Order (today known as the Order of Friars Minor). It is said that as he died on the night of May 20, 1444 outside the city of Aquila, he requested to be placed on the bare earth as Francis had at his own death.

He had a complicated relationship with the Church's leadership. In 1426 Bernardine was summoned to Rome to defend himself against charges of heresy for his promotion of the devotion to the Holy Name of Jesus, something of a novel devotion. He was eventually acquitted, but Bernardine's innovative efforts in the realm of pastoral ministry reflect the ongoing struggle that members of religious orders often face while balancing the needs of the people and what is often viewed as immutable tradition.

Popular Preaching: Inspiration for Franciscans Today

That for which Bernardine is best remembered stands as a model for Franciscans today. Popular preaching is perhaps one of the greatest needs the Church has in our own age. How often do you hear a terrible homily? Sure, preaching within the context of the Mass is one area that Bernardine's example could be followed in responding to the concerns of the day in light of Christian faith, but what also set Bernardine apart was the way in which he lived what he preached and spoke about faith in a variety of settings.

Preaching in the fifteenth century wasn't quite the same as it is today, both in its style and in its relationship with the celebration of the Eucharist – there was oftentimes a distinction between the two, preaching was at times more of a public civil event than a liturgical one. Nevertheless, responding to the concerns of the day in a way that connects to people in an intelligent and faithful way continues to be something that Franciscans are known for today (I think of Holy Name Province's own *Ministry of the Word*, for example) and remains our challenge to carry on. I have heard from many women and men around our province that they travel many miles, past many other churches to worship at our urban ministry centers, parishes and college chapels in part because of the preaching and welcome.

On a more personal note, I find Bernardine's example in balancing academic study and popular preaching to be a model for those friars in education ministry. Mormando writes, "Bernardino's speech is at once both learned and colloquial, constantly oscillating in its syntax and idiom between the language of the marketplace and that of the medieval classroom." In my own ministry as a Friar Minor I strive to strike this balance too. Through my writing I try to reach both popular and academic audiences, albeit in different ways. On one hand, my first book, scheduled to come out next spring, is published by a popular press and is aimed at providing a contemporary look at Franciscan spirituality for a broad audience in a manner not unlike some of my articles that have appeared in magazines like *America* or *St. Anthony Messenger*. On the other hand, I have published several peer-reviewed and very technical scholarly papers in top theological journals like *The Heythrop Journal* and *Worship*. While I work hard on research that is presented at academic conferences, I have also given retreats and public lectures to general audiences. This both/and approach reflects the Franciscan model of Bernardine.

Bernardine was in a sense an innovator who, while well versed in the even-then slightly antiquated form of medieval preaching, drew on contemporary images, metaphors and examples to make his sermons relevant and understandable. I believe that Franciscans, following in Bernardine's footprints, need to look for and embrace new forms of communicating the Gospel message to all people.

As the Pope and the United States bishops have in recent months cautiously encouraged, the new social media are becoming increasingly more vital in communicating in today's world. In order for the next generation to hear the Franciscan voice, Franciscans must meet people where they are – which is the very definition of popular preaching. I have experienced this first hand in the increasingly popularity of my blog, *DatingGod.org*, which started with several hundred readers a day and has increased to at times several thousand a day.

I am firmly committed to the belief that Franciscan preaching – in its varied forms, both liturgical and otherwise – must be done in both the academy of professional theologians and in the public squares of everyday life. Franciscan theology and spirituality, that particular take on the Gospel life as first modeled by St. Francis and St. Clare, offers the Church and world an always timely renewal of Christian living. We, like St. Bernardine of Siena, must rise to the vocational challenge to preach the Gospel in all manner of life, ministry and word.

May 18, 2011

11

Rebuilding the Church like Francis

The San Damiano Cross spoke to Francis's heart near the

beginning of his conversion away from a life of selfishness and toward God and others. Christ's message for the one-day saint is Christ's message for us today: "Rebuild my Church!"

Francis of Assisi at first took this command from God to be a call to carpentry and masonry, constructing a building brick-by-brick. But soon Francis came to realize that rebuilding the Church had little to do with making sure that this or that building's roof didn't leak. Instead, Francis remembered that when we speak of "The Church" we are never talking about a place, property, or *thing*. Nope. The Church is the Body of Christ, which is a community of all the baptized. That's right, you, me, your friends, your family, everyone (even people you don't like). *We* are the Body of Christ, the Church, and Christ's mission for us, as it was for Francis 800-years-ago, is that we work to rebuild it.

What does this mean for us? I suggest that it means that reformation is not such a dirty word. Every now and then in the history of the Church, this is especially true in recent decades, the term "reform" has come to mean less-than-favorable things in certain circles. But, many reformers have been hailed as saints and extraordinary people. This includes figures like St. Francis of Assisi, St. Paul, Gregory the Great, Pope John XXIII, and so on. What makes these folks so important is that they served as prophets in their time, seeking to rebuild the Body of Christ.

One rebuilds the Church when he or she is an instrument of reform. This doesn't necessarily mean protest or "doing something new," in fact it means quite the opposite. Literally, "reformation" means to re-form something, to *return* to the original form after it has been *de*formed in some way. The great reformers, those who are master constructors of the Church see with the eyes of the Spirit those things that no longer fit the *form* of the Gospel Life. In an effort to live out the authentic call of discipleship, a reformer must be committed to his or her baptismal call as a member of the Body of Christ.

This is what Francis of Assisi did. His reform stems from his desire to do one thing: live according to the Gospel of our Lord Jesus Christ. Sounds simple enough, but the consequences are staggering and have changed the world. He constantly shed those elements of popular faith and culture that were *deformations* of the Church, the Body of Christ. The first instance of this is when he embraced the leper. Lepers were outside the community, destined to be marginalized without voice, power or recognition. Both the civil authorities and the Church authorities of the day endorsed this type of treatment. For Francis, the symbolic beginning of his reforming is when he moved beyond the normative boundaries that separated people, that broke and injured the Body of Christ and instead became a (re)builder of that broken Body, gathering those who are pushed to the edges of society back into the embrace of love that symbolizes the loving embrace with which God created this world.

On this day when we pause to recall the model of exemplary Christian living in the life and ministry of Francis of Assisi, we would do well to listen to Christ's mission for us today as Francis listened to Christ's mission for him some eight centuries ago.

Become rebuilders of the Church, the Body of Christ. Be a reformer that moves beyond the boundaries of prejudice and discrimination, ignorance and misunderstanding. Be like St. Francis, open and loving to all.

October 4, 2010

12

Robert Grosseteste:
The Greatest Theologian You (Probably) Don't Know

I was reminded in an email exchange yesterday of how much I really love Robert Grosseteste, the thirteenth-century theologian, one of the early chancellors of the young Oxford University and, finally, Bishop of Lincoln (in the UK). In addition to those three jobs — each of which would be worthy of accolades and recollection in their own right — he was also the first instructor of theology for the earliest Franciscan friars to arrive on the island of England even during Francis of Assisi's own lifetime.

Grosseteste was a genius — hands down! In addition to the "sacred sciences" — namely theology and philosophy, Grosseteste was also a passionate scientist (insofar as that term is not used anachronistically by our own standards of the profession). He wrote on optics, light, and other phenomena centuries before the scientific method and the natural sciences as we know them today were born. His interests were manifold and his influence was far-reaching. Not only did his work influence generations of Franciscans in England, but his thought helped shape the theological outlook of Franciscans and others in Paris and elsewhere as well.

His most famous text is probably the small treatise *De Luce* ("On Light"). At the risk of sounding overly romantic, it was *De Luce* that first led me to fall in love with this eight-hundred-year-old theologian's work. It is simply poetic and the theological content latent in his bold scientific efforts in cosmology is wonderfully inspiring. I am also convinced that in *De Luce* Grosseteste makes an argument that sounds a lot like an early version of the Big Bang Theory (advanced by yet another cleric some centuries later, George Lemaitre, a Roman Catholic priest and scientist)... but that's for another day.

I have always found myself much more interested in the medieval thinkers of the Oxford school than those of Paris. This is, likely because, as scholars like C.F.J. Martin and others keenly point out, Paris was much more tightly controlled in terms of curricula and what was being read and taught. In the late thirteenth century it was Paris that experienced the Aristotelian condemnations and other forms of resource-prohibition, while Oxford experienced no such limitations. Thinkers like Grosseteste were free to theologize and intellectually explore uncharted territory, albeit in at-times unusual or idiosyncratic ways. Nevertheless, the originality most usually associated with medieval figures like Scotus and Ockham begins much earlier in the life and work of their brilliant predecessor, Robert Grosseteste.

Here is a little snippet (I wish I could share the whole text!) from Grosseteste's *Hexaëmeron* ("On the Six Days of Creation"), taken from the first chapter of the first part of the treatise. It is here that he begins his reflection on the biblical account of creation found in Genesis. His starting point is richly Christocentric and reflects an ecclesiology that would make both St. Paul and St. Augustine very proud, all the while elucidating — if briefly — his understanding of theology. It's great.

> Each science, each kind of wisdom has a matter and a subject on which its attention is turned. Hence this most sacred wisdom, whose name is theology, has a subject on which it is turned. That subject is thought by some to be the whole Christ: that is to say, the incarnate Word, together with his body, the Church. Or perhaps it would not be unfitting to say that the subject of this wisdom is that One of which the Saviour himself speaks in the gospel of John: "and not for them only do I pray, but for them also who through their word shall believe in me; that they all may be one, as thou, Father, in me, and I in thee; that they also may be on in us; that the world may believe that thou hast sent me." In this One then, of which it was said "that they also may be one in us" there seem to be grouped together the following unities or unions:

> [1] The union by which the incarnate Word is one Christ, on Christ in his person, God and man; [2] the union by which Christ is one in nature with the church through the human nature he took on; [3] and the union by which the church is reunited with him by a condign taking up, in the sacrament of the Eucharist, of that flesh which he lookup form the virgin, in which he was crucified, died and was buried, rose from the dead and ascended into heaven, from whence he will come to judge the living and the dead.

> These three unions seem to be grouped together in the One which is called the whole Christ. (Grosseteste, *Hexaëmeron*, 1.1.1.)

For those who are eager to learn more about Robert Grosseteste, check out the "Electronic Grosseteste," a website created by the scholar Jim Ginther at St. Louis University. You can find more about his biography and some easily accessible Latin editions of his writings.

October 26, 2011

13

A Lesser-Known Franciscan View of Creation

I bet that most people think of Francis of Assisi's *Canticle of the Creatures* when they think of a Franciscan view of creation. Some might think of the theological view of creation found in St. Bonaventure's work, particularly in his description of creation as God's vestige. Others might recall John Duns Scotus's understanding of *haecceity* and the uniqueness of each and every dimension of creation.

But most folks, even professed Franciscans, would probably not think of Friar Jacopone da Todi (c. 1230-1306) and see his collection of medieval lauds as a resource for Franciscan spirituality of the environment.

Among his many lauds stands one that strikes me as worthy of special reflection with regard to this theme. In this particular poem, we see how Jacopone expresses the potential to see God in all creation through the senses. The laud portrays a richly Christocentric view of creation and this ability to see the Creator in the created — truly a mark of Franciscan spirituality.

How The Soul Through the Senses
Finds God in All Creatures

By Br. Jacopone da Todi

O Love, divine Love,
why do You lay siege to me?
In a frenzy of love for me, You find no rest.
From five sides You move against me,
Hearing, sight, taste, touch, and scent.
To come out is to be caught; I cannot hide from You.

If I come out through sight I see
Love Painted in every form and color,
Inviting me to come to You, to dwell in You.
If I leave through the door of hearing,
What I hear points only to You, Lord;
I cannot escape Love through this gate.
If I come out through taste, every flavor proclaims:
"Love, divine Love, hungering Love!
You have caught me on Your hook, for You want to reign in me."
If I leave through the door of scent I sense You in all creation;
You have caught me And wounded me through that fragrance.
If I come out through the sense of touch
I find Your lineaments in every creature;
To try to flee from You is madness.
Love, I flee from You, afraid to give You my heart;
I see that You make me one with You,
I cease to be me and can no longer find myself.
If I see evil in a man or defect or temptation, You fuse me with him, and make me suffer;
O Love without limits, who is it You love?
It is You, O Crucified Christ,
Who take possession of me,
Drawing me out of the sea to the shore;
There I suffer to see Your wounded heart.
Why did You endure the pain? So that I might be healed.

November 29, 2010

14

A Franciscan Perspective on Labor Day

"Let the brothers who know how to work do so and exercise that trade they have learned, provided it is not contrary to the good of their souls and can be performed honestly" (St. Francis, *Regula non Bullata*

VII:3).

Work has always played a significant role in the life of the Friars Minor. In each of the two written forms of the nascent Franciscan way of life, or Rules, Francis makes it clear that the brothers are to work. Unlike the monastic communities and, perhaps, secular clergy (i.e., medieval 'diocesan' clergy) that would have relied on endowments, land-use payments, and other forms of income, the friars were to earn their own way. This was, in the beginning, imagined by Francis as the continuation of whatever trade the new brothers previously practiced. If you were a carpenter, then you would continue to work with wood as a friar; If you were a teacher, then you would continue to teach as a friar; and so on. The only restriction was that the brothers could not work in a trade that was sinful or unjust.

This way of understanding work centered on the two-fold emphasis of Franciscan spirituality: the dignity of the individual vocation of each person as created by God (there is no "universal" or "singular" set of skills and gifts, but, as St. Paul explains in Scripture, there are many iterations of the Spirit in the lives of Christians) and friars were not to be "professional religious," but were to live in solidarity with ordinary people.

Perhaps the foremost scholar on Franciscan work and labor is the friar David Flood, OFM, whose recent work is titled, *The Daily Labor of the Early Franciscans* (Franciscan Institute Publications, 2010). Here is a short excerpt from the text, if you are interested in learning more about the Franciscan approach to labor and work, be sure to check out the full text.

> Francis and his companions began by working and soon formulated their own policy on work. In their original written agreement, once they had rid themselves of the possessions and relations that integrated them into society, they had to determine a new way of providing themselves with the means of life and of relating to other people. That caused them no problem: they intended to work and said so in a simple phrase. They worked at trades, those who had

one, and the helped out in the poorhouses and leprosaria that dotted the countryside. They worked well, in the élan of their new life together, and they took little as pay: no money, simply the things they needed. Initially that was very little. Furthermore, they also defined their relations to other people. They set out to wish people peace, to share with them, and not to fight over material goods and pursue social position. (5-6)

On this day dedicated to celebrating labor and work, recalling that so many are struggling to find dignified opportunities to work, may we return to the Franciscan approach to work as an inherent right and duty. May we, like those early brothers, work well, seeking only what we need and not more. May we, like those early brothers, not seek social position, but share our lives with one another freely and openly. May God bless you on this labor day.

September 5, 2011

15

Angela the Mystic: Follow Christ, Adopt Divine Poverty

The Thirteenth-Century Franciscan mystic, Angela of Foligno explains in her book *Instructions* that in order to be a Christian, one must supplant the 'false poverty' of fallen humanity with the 'divine poverty.'

This God and man Jesus Christ raised us up and redeemed us by poverty. His poverty was truly ineffable, for it concealed so much of his total power and nobility. He let himself be blasphemed, vilified, verbally abused, seized, dragged, scourged, and crucified, and through it all, he always behaved as one powerless to help himself. His poverty is a model for our life; we should follow this example. For our part, we do not have to hide our power, for we have none; but we must manifest and be aware of our great powerlessness.

It should strike those familiar with the Franciscan tradition that poverty stands as a central element in one's spiritual outlook. Beginning with the Incarnation, the symbol of God's kenosis, we can recognize the poverty of God. Divine poverty, as Angela calls it, is perhaps better described as evangelical poverty, following the Gospel life.

The powerlessness that Angela attributes to Christ as the model for our lives reflects the foolishness of God that Paul writes about in his epistolary and that which St. Francis of Assisi embraced as something of a motto. Simplicity, humility, selflessness are the attributes of those who follow the one who empties Himself totally for us, the God-made-flesh.

False poverty is the ignorance that leads human beings to sin, the blindness that self-centeredness and greed inflict on the people created *imago Dei*. But the embrace of a way of life after the example of God revealed fully in Christ lifts us up, as Angela puts it, to a place where we recognize our indebtedness to God, our ultimate humility in the face of our self-importance and our real calling to serve one another in love.

Only then, following Christ through adopting divine or evangelical poverty, are we able to bear the name Christian. For it is then that we become Christ-like.

February 18, 2011

PART 2

CHRISTIAN NONVIOLENCE
AND PEACEMAKING

16

Christians Ought to be Pacifists

Today is the feast of "The Holy Innocents," the day that traditionally commemorates the children murdered under King Herod's order to kill all those under two years of age in an effort to prevent the prophecy of the coming messiah. The scriptural source for this day is found in Matthew's Gospel (2:16-18), with very little additional information to supplement this narrative by way of extra biblical resources (the first non-Christian reference to this decree doesn't appear until some four centuries after the fact).

Nevertheless, I think it is wholly appropriate to reflect on a day that marks the innocent loss of life at the hand of military personnel following a ruler's command. Generally, I believe that many pastors and bloggers tend to dwell on the fact that the narrative is centered on the murder of children, and, as you can already anticipate, some have appropriated the event for so-called "pro-life" (read: anti-abortion) polemics.

I, too, feel that this feast day is perfectly suited for pro-life reflections, just not in the same way that my brothers and sisters in faith who might choose to stand in front of Planned Parenthood and hate both the sin and sinner would. It seems to me that we might instead look at the broader designation of the feast, for which the day's title reads: "Holy *Innocents*," and not children or unborn, and so forth. Instead, it is a commemoration of the loss of *all* innocent life, a true call to reflect on the ways in which Christianity is most authentically "pro-life" in all forms.

Today I feel compelled to reflect on how Christians ought be pacifists.

The innocent loss of life in war and war-related violent enterprises should be enough to compel all people to vow against violence in any form, but Christians — for whom a God who enters the worlds and surrenders to the death penalty rather than violently resist is a non-negotiable element of faith — really have little choice.

My interest in this theme as the centerpiece of today's

reflection comes from a recent article in the Huffington Post titled, "Should Christians be Pacifists?" by Rev. Candace Chellew-Hodge. Published the day after Christmas, it continues to draw on the theme of the season — God's entrance into the world as one like us: a human being — while responding to some rather absurd remarks by representatives of the American Family Association, a conservative "Christian" 501(c)3 organization committed to their mission statement, which reads: "The American Family Association exists to motivate and equip individuals to restore American culture to its moral foundations." (Again, I think these folks would be surprised to discover the "moral foundations" of secular liberal philosophers like Jefferson and Washington who authored the founding documents of this nation, while owning slaves and treating women and children like chattel).

The impetus for Chellew-Hodge's article was the remark of the AFA's director, Bryan Fischer, who said that the awarding of the Medal of Honor to "Army Sgt. Salvatore Giunta for saving lives during a battle in Afghanistan has 'feminized' the award." He goes on:

> So the question is this: when are we going to start awarding the Medal of Honor once again for soldiers who kill people and break things so our families can sleep safely at night? I would suggest our culture has become so feminized that we have become squeamish at the thought of the valor that is expressed in killing enemy soldiers through acts of bravery. We know instinctively that we should honor courage, but shy away from honoring courage if it results in the taking of life rather than in just the saving of life. So we find it safe to honor those who throw themselves on a grenade to save their buddies.

What makes matters worse, Chellew-Hodge observed, is that Fischer claims: "Christianity is not a religion of pacifism."

Fischer couldn't be further from the truth. Without rehearsing the entirety of ante-Nicene Christian history and Scriptural support for obligatory Christian pacifism (after Constantine and the reversal of power that came with religious tolerance and then the state religion — religion had to justify power and with imperial power, violence) – Chellew-Hodge does a nice job with examples from the Church Fathers in her article — I will say that there is no justification in the earliest Christian tradition for Christian-endorsed violence. So-called "just war theory," was a later development rooted in Augustinian philosophical reflection that had, after the marriage of state and religion, to justify the state's use of violence in its own interest. A move Christ could never endorse.

Francis of Assisi. Martin Luther King, Jr. Maximilian Kolbe. John Howard Yoder. Stanley Hauerwas. Jesus of Nazareth. And many, many other names come to mind when the theme of Christian pacifism arises. The most celebrated figures in Christianity have always been avowed pacifists. What other choice does a Christian have?

December 28, 2010

17

Violence and Film: A Struggle for Me

We all grow and mature, not just as human beings in emotional, physical, spiritual, and intellectual capacities, but also in spiritual and theological ways.

In recent years something that has become more and more apparent to me is the way in which violence permeates our society and our social interactions, sometimes in ways that seem superficially innocuous, many of these forms of subtextual violence undergird what the philosopher James K. A. Smith has called "secular liturgies," such as the 'shopping mall' or 'American nationalism.'

Entertainment also fits the bill. The way in which sexuality and violence form the gravitational center of our visual (TV, movies) and audial (popular music) entertainment has increasingly come to my attention as I become more aware of the incompatibility of violence and Christianity in terms of theology, ethics and praxis. As a Franciscan friar, nonviolence is very much at the core of my religious charism (as I, personally, would argue is true for all of Christianity).

How then can I make sense of violence and film? Is there an ethical imperative placed on Christians, or at least Franciscans, to abstain from watching films that one knows will certainly contain violent imagery? What about historically based films, is there a distinction that should be made between historical narrative and gratuitous exploitation for the sake of industry economics?

Last night I saw the film "Hannah." For months I have been intrigued by the trailers for the film, captivated by the story of a young girl who, living with her father in some place of absolute remoteness, is sent on a mission by herself. She is a skilled — what's the word... assassin? — who, as the film reveals, is out to avenge her mother's murder.

At age 15, she has never met someone other than her father nor experienced music, electricity, or any other comfort of modern life. Yet, her father has trained her in martial arts, combat, marksmanship; and all sorts of scientific, geographic, and historical information. She speaks many languages and, on one hand, exhibits the highest degree of intelligence. On the other hand, she has little to no social or cultural intelligence (which sets up some rather cute scenes including one with a teenage boy and a potential first kiss).

I rather liked the film. Aside from some very poor screenwriting for secondary characters (anytime someone in a suit opens his or her mouth, the most listless and unoriginal dialogue follows), the story was creative – provided you can suspend your disbelief long enough to follow the bait. (I had to consciously be aware of that need, there were pragmatic questions that kept arising for me, like: "if they are isolated in the artic forest, where do they get fuel for their lamps? In light of that isolation, what happened when the 15-year-old Hannah came of age? Not too many pharmacies or grocery stores around for dad or Hannah to pick-up feminine products).

But what troubles me, at least in some inchoate way, is whether or not it is ethically 'ok' to enjoy such entertainment that relies so heavily on violence, notions of revenge, and other themes contrary to the call to live the Gospel life and proclaim the Kingdom of God.

How does one draw the line? What film doesn't contain

some sort of violence? Would "Star Wars" be off limits? What about the classical films of American culture — The "Godfather" series, for example?

I am not sure that I have an answer to this inquiry, but it is something I will continue to explore. One thing is for certain, the degree to which violence operates below the surface of so much of our popular entertainment is staggering. Perhaps what is needed is an acute awareness of that reality, what is called for is the discomfort I felt in the experience of the tension that pulls at the conscience of a Christian who recognizes the incongruity of popular entertainment and the human call to be live as *Imago Dei*.

What do you think?

April 9, 2011

18

The Death Penalty is Not an Ethical Matter

Well, now that you've picked yourself up off the floor, having fallen down from the seeming absurdity of this essay's title, I'd like to make two arguments to support this claim that the death penalty is not an ethical matter. The first is simple and, perhaps, not all that convincing; namely, that this is a "no brainer" and really shouldn't have to be subjected to the sorts of debating that it is prone to initiate. In this sense, what I might call the common-sense argument seems to suffice for a certain percentage of the population that recognizes the state-exercised executions are wrong.

The second argument I'd like to introduce here, although I doubt I can fully exhaust the complicated aspects in need of elucidation in this short overview, is that I believe capital punishment should be categorized as intrinsically evil. For those unfamiliar with that distinction, it (in a nutshell) means that it is an act that is always and everywhere already wrong, there are no exceptions. Two of the most well-known examples of intrinsically evil actions are abortion and torture. Neither are ever permitted according to Catholic moral teaching, one could never — so the determining category posits — imagine a circumstance when the action is morally justifiable.

The thing is that these distinctions are often argued within the realm of moral theology and ethics. What makes something morally right or wrong can become a juridical exercise that weighs evidence from a variety of sources and angles. There is a casuistry-inclined bent to some of this analysis that focuses on all the possible circumstances under which such an action might take place and considers the myriad factors involved, all in the effort to establish a universal norm by which to understand the inherent moral value of the given act.

There is nothing inherently wrong with the moral theological approach, but sitting in the Director's Guild Theatre in Manhattan yesterday afternoon to listen to *The New Yorker Festival* panel on Capital Punishment, I came to realize that maybe this was not the most helpful theological approach toward discerning the moral value or ethical category of the death penalty. I think that an alternative approach might be from the angle of a more foundational theological category, exploring the Christian understanding of the human person (theological anthropology) as the primary focus of the evil of capital punishment.

Granted, theological anthropology plays a major role in moral theological discussions, but I wonder if a closer look at our understanding of the human person might offer an *a priori* argument — beyond just a contribution to the circumstantial adjudication of the ethical variety — for the death penalty as an intrinsically evil act.

One of the ways I have been considering this reevaluation of the method used to categorize the death penalty, rooted perhaps in my own Franciscan tradition, is the purpose of the Decalogue. The Ten Commandments are often (if not only ever) presented as moral laws, a juridical "bottom line" by which all people are to live. "Thou shall not kill" is understood as a proscription against murder. Yet, following the theological foundations of Francis of Assisi's *Canticle of the Creatures* in which the saint does not establish a legal code, but offers a descriptive reflection on what is *inherently* human, just as warmth and light are inherent properties of fire.

What if the so-called "second tablet" of the decalogue was not understood as a regulatory list of laws to be followed, but an anthropological description of what it means to be human? Instead of listing the things that we are "not permitted to do," the Ten Commandments are descriptors that elucidate the meaning of our being *Imago Dei*. Instead of saying, "you should not do X," a way of reading this dimension of Divine Revelation is, "you are most fully human when living X," X in this case referring to the vision of life proffered by the one who reflects the just relationships modeled in the decalogue.

An understanding that it is unhuman to take another's life regardless of the circumstances ("thou shall not kill" does not include a single qualifier... e.g., "thou shall not kill...unless he/she is a really bad person or you are at war"), offers a categorical rejection of the notion that one could ever present an argument in which one has the "right" or is "justified" in the execution of another. No one has the "right" to kill, which is why a murderer should indeed be punished, should have rights curbed, and not be granted access to the rest of society for its safety and for the murder's penalty.

But to suggest that what would be the correct punitive action for even the most egregious crimes is the taking of yet another human life would seem to fly in the face of what it means to be authentically human. In this regard such a calculated and deliberate action such as is the case in capital punishment actually reflects a failure of society to live up to its inherent identity as a community of human persons and of individuals who reject, through their individual sense of retributive justice, their very identity as a human person created *Imago Dei*.

I believe that there is a lot more that can be said on this, which requires more space and time than I have here today. I wanted to toss some of these thoughts out there for discussion as I continue to consider how the prohibition of capital punishment and the death penalty as an intrinsically evil act can be understood as arising out of who we are as human persons rather than from the perspective of moral-theological evaluation or even a political-policy consideration.

As it happens, all of this reflection occurs around the same time a news story about capital punishment and Catholic moral teaching comes out of the Vatican ("Dead Wrong: Catholic Must No Longer Support Capital Punishment") and *The New Yorker Festival* featured the panel I attended ("Capital Punishment: Is the Death Penalty Dying?"). Our age calls for more creative and innovative thinking about these pressing theological and social matters.

October 2, 2011

19

Justice is Never Served with the Death Penalty

"Justice has been served for Officer Mark MacPhail and his family," state Attorney General Sam Olens said in a statement, According to the *Washington Post*. A falser statement could not have been said. That is, at least from the perspective of Christianity we cannot say that justice has been served in the state execution of Troy Davis. I would also argue that it's not only religious women and men, such as Roman Catholics, who rightly claim that state-sponsored executions are unjust and archaic, but most of the post-industrial world also rejects capital punishment.

The United States remains one of only two (with Japan) such "First-World" powers that legally permits the death penalty. The recent case of Troy Davis and the State of Georgia is only the latest, and tragic, illustration of why this form of punishment must end.

The case of Davis is perhaps the most visible instance of anti-death penalty support in the United States in some years. The *Washington Post* reports:

> Hundreds of thousands of people signed petitions on Davis' behalf, and prominent supporters included an ex-president and an ex-FBI director, liberals and conservatives. His attorneys said seven of nine key witnesses against him disputed all or parts of their

testimony, but state and federal judges repeatedly ruled against him — three times on Wednesday alone.

Davis asked his friends and family to "continue to fight this fight." Of prison officials he said, "May God have mercy on your souls. May God bless your souls."

The case for which Davis had been sentenced to death remains a murky one. The legitimacy of the guilty verdict has consistently been called into question in more-than-a-decade since he was convicted, in large part due to the dissolution of the State's case against Davis and the shifting stories from witnesses upon whose testimony much of Davis's sentencing relied. The *New York Times* recaps the events:

> Mr. Davis was convicted of the 1989 shooting of Officer MacPhail, who was working a second job as a security guard. A homeless man called for help after a group that included Mr. Davis began to assault him, according to court testimony. When Officer MacPhail went to assist him, he was shot in the face and the heart.

> Before Wednesday, Mr. Davis had walked to the brink of execution three times.

> His conviction came after testimony by some witnesses who later recanted and on the scantest of physical evidence, adding fuel to those who rely on the Internet to rally against executions and to question the validity of eyewitness identification and of the court system itself.

While much of the protesting of the death penalty in the case of Davis is rooted in the particularity of his case, namely the sand upon which the foundation of his conviction stands, I want to remind Christians that even if the preponderance of evidence was overwhelmingly in favor of conviction, justice would not be served in the death penalty.

The United States Catholic Bishops have repeatedly spoken out against capital punishment in the US. The fact that the United States continues to permit, in some states, the murder (which is the deliberate killing of another human being) of women and men, regardless of what crimes they have committed, only supports and perpetuates what John Paul II famously referred to as "the culture of death," a phrase that is popular among anti-abortion protesters.

Although it is often subordinated in popular Catholic circles to abortion and other life issues, the death penalty is an egregious transgression against the dignity and sanctity of all human life. Pope John Paul II said as much when he visited St. Louis in 1999: "A sign of hope is the increasing recognition that the dignity of human life must never be taken away, even in the case of someone who has done great evil. Modern society has the means of protecting itself, without definitively denying criminals the chance to reform. I renew the appeal I made most recently at Christmas for a consensus to end the death penalty, which is both cruel and unnecessary."

The archbishop of Atlanta, who is the metropolitan bishop of the state that executed Troy Davis last night, has also publicly spoken out against the death penalty, such as in 2008 when he gave an address on the subject at Emory University.

One year after the reintroduction of the death penalty in the United States (1976), the late Cardinal Bernardin of Chicago, then president of the USCCB, wrote the first of several USCCB statements against the death penalty. A wise paragraph of that 1977 document is worth quoting at length here:

> I do not challenge society's right to punish the capital offender, but I would ask all to examine the question of whether there are other and better approaches to protecting our people from violent crimes than resorting to executions. In particular I ask those who advocate the use of capital punishment to reflect prayerfully upon all the moral dimensions of the issue. It is not so much a matter of whether an argument can be advanced in favor of the death penalty; such arguments have already been forcefully made by many people of evident good will, although

others find them less than convincing. But the more pertinent question at this time in our history is what course of action best fosters that respect for life, all human life, in a society such as ours in which such respect is so sadly lacking. In my view, more destruction of human life is not what America needs in 1977.

I think Cardinal Bernardin hit the nail on the head. All the death penalty does is add more destruction of human life in our communities, nation and world. Either we are for life or we are against it. Justice is never served with the death penalty.

September 22, 2011

20

Love Your Enemies.
No Really, Love Your Enemies

I thought I'd share a passage from St. Francis's *Earlier Rule* (*Regula non bullata*) Chapter XXII in which those who seek to follow in the footprints of the Saint from Assisi in living the Gospel Life must take to heart the command of the Lord.

> All my brothers; let us pay attention to what the Lord says: Love your enemies and do good to those who hate you (Mt 5:44) for our Lord Jesus Christ, Whose footprints we must follow, called His betrayer a friend and willingly offered Himself to His executioners

> Our friends, therefore are all those who unjustly inflict upon us distress and anguish, shame and injury, sorrow and punishment, martyrdom and death. We must love them greatly for we shall possess eternal life because of what they bring us. (*ER* XXII:1-4)

These are not easy words to hear, especially in a political and ecclesiastical climate that is marked by hostility and polarization, something, at times, to which I find myself succumbing unwittingly. My guess is that most of us revel in hating or despising our 'enemies,' justifying our disgust or disregard of others with the so-called logic or wisdom of the world. Perhaps it's time to embrace the *Theologos*, the wisdom of God who is Christ. In doing so, may we follow the example of the little poor man from Assisi who models this way of living for us.

January 13, 2012

21

The Violent Power of Words: A Franciscan's Response

In the beginning of this weekend was a word. And this word was not of God and this word was not God.

This word was legion, not singular, and it was divisive, caustic, disrespectful and violent — both in substance and, as we so unfortunately witnessed, in effect.

At this point I have become entirely disenchanted with the "he said, she said" pseudo-conversations that have filled the cable-news airwaves for the better part of today. I will be very honest and say that I do not wish to indict anyone other than the gunman as the immediate cause of Saturday's tragedy.

However, as the Greek philosophical tradition — appropriated as it has been by the medieval theological synthesis and passed on to us today — makes very, very clear, there oftentimes several causes in an act.

No one will dispute the mental instability of Saturday's gunman, something for which not even the "Tea Party messiah" Glenn Beck (a title bestowed to him in a Vanity Fair article I read today) nor his kindred spirit Sarah Palin could be responsible. But the contemporary political climate marked as it is by the increasingly vitriolic discourse, violent imagery, and disrespectful rhetoric should not be so easily dismissed, regardless whether it is or isn't the direct impetus for that young man's murderous action.

The use of words in this country is a problem and,

tangential as it may be presented by those who defended firearm cross-hair diagrams and violent rallying cries, it has made this country and the world less safe and has turned our civic arena into a veritable tinderbox of fear and distrust.

As the adage goes, it is true that sticks and stones (and bullets) break bones, but (contrary to popular belief) words are actually much more powerful. It is through propaganda, the cunning use of language and narrative that political messages are conveyed to the masses.

Some will say that it is the violent action that needs to be the focus, but such people neglect the significance of a hostile environment saturated in fear. Those who defend the public discourse of late offer a myopic reading of twentieth-century history that discards European, African, and Asian genocide and war. Words, language, violent imagery are what was used to capitalize on the fear and uncertainty of post-war Germany. Hitler (as Joe Nangle elegantly noted in the last post on this blog) did not rise to power by force, he was put into power because of the political milieu that arose from deliberate use of words.

Violent, hostile, and divisive words are the seeds of violent, hostile, and divisive action, planted in the collective and particular psyche of a nation's citizenry. Rush Limbaugh argued earlier today that his and others' discursive styles are not a problem because shootings — like the one that took the life of 6 people, including a 9-year-old girl, and wounded 20 others — are the "exception" to the rule and if vitriolic and violently hyperbolic language was *really* a problem, then there would be shootings everyday.

Such absurdity and defense of an indefensible position continues to enable the cycle of violence, fear, and distrust among the country and world's populations. Need I even mention the outbreak of bullying in our schools this year and the tragic suicides that followed — so much for irrelevance of words!

I was deliberate in my Johannine allusion above. The reason I wanted to capture your attention with that implied reference to the prologue of John's Gospel is to dramatically draw your attention back to the centrality of the word (*logos*) in Christianity. It doesn't simply begin in John, but the creation and wisdom tradition of the Hebrew Scriptures (Old Testament) also frequently refer to the "word of God" as God's creative and redemptive action in this world.

How we use words is very, very important. Words are revelatory, they show us something that was previously unseen. They make present a reality that was not present prior to their speaking or being written. THE Word did this for God, the Incarnation revealed to us God as God had never before shown us — it is decisive, it is complete, it is indeed Holy.

The way we use words should take on similar sanctity. I will be the first in line to admit that my use of words has, as often as they can be comforting or edifying, also been caustic and hurtful. For those who have ever experienced that from me, know that I continue to apologize. However, I know that what I have done in those occasional instances *is wrong* and will not defend my behavior. That is what is, to begin with, what we need from those political and media figures who refuse to admit their use of words has been wrong and is, in some part, responsible for the mess that we find ourselves in today.

This mess is not just a shooting in Arizona, but the political and cultural ethos of animosity, vitriol, and disrespect.

St. Francis of Assisi actually has much to say to us today in these political matters. In his famous *Canticle of the Creatures,* Francis first mentions human beings within the context of peacemaking and forgiveness. For the Italian saint, to be human is to be a peacemaker, ushering in the Kingdom as God had in Christ. That verse arose as Francis's response to a political battle involving the Mayor and the Bishop of Assisi. Where are our peacemakers in the political arena today to remind Palin, Beck, and others that to be human is to make peace and to do so with *both* actions and words?

In another place, his *Letter to all the Faithful,* Francis wrote:

Let us, moreover, bring forth fruits worthy of penance. And let us love our neighbors as ourselves, and, if anyone does not wish to love them as himself [or herself] or cannot, let him [or her] at least do them no harm, but let him [or her] do good to them.

Acknowledging the reality that not all can live up to God's

commandment to love one another, Francis exhorts all those who call themselves "Christian" to at least do no harm. This includes our words.

Our choice of language does indeed have consequences and these consequences cannot be ignored. No one who dares to bear the name "Christian" can speak about his or her brother or sister in Christ the way so many self-professed faithful have in recent years, months, and weeks. It is time to remember the meaning of conversion and live it.

January 10, 2011

22

Guns in America:
Insecurity Compensation to the Extreme!

So I've been thinking a lot about firearms this week. I imagine that I'm not alone. For one thing, several legislators — on both state and federal levels — have made public statements about the greater need for gun legislation.

The NRA, as some commentators have duly noted, has remained silent on the subject of their existential theme. Meanwhile some "conservative commentators" have defended their ongoing interpretation of the second amendment to the United States Constitution that, within the context of establishing a well-ordered militia (ostensibly to defend a fledgling republic against aggressive imperial powers like England...centuries ago), guarantees the right of citizens to be armed. In such a case, this amendment is read in the most liberal light with its interpreters claiming it allows for an unmitigated permission for the average citizen to own and wield his or her choice of a weapon of (at least some, if not mass) destruction.

What the hell?

Prepared as I am for the criticisms that will inevitably land in my inbox from those who think that I am "unpatriotic," or something of the sort, I simply say that I am honored to be so labeled if it means that my public challenge is unsettling those who need to be unsettled and upsetting those who are comfortable with the way things currently stand.

I believe that the second amendment has been grievously misinterpreted for decades, if not centuries. I find no reason to repeal the law, believing wholeheartedly that what it says is indeed justifiable — and here's the key — *when read in context!* The text reads: "A well regulated militia, being necessary to the security of a free state, the right of the people to keep and bear arms, shall not be infringed."

While I wish we lived in a world where a "well regulated militia" was not necessary and war was nothing but a memory of a less-civil and unchristian time, I accept that our military (of which my father is a Marine Corps veteran) is not going anywhere. And, in order to have a military that exists practically in this world, the right for soldiers to bear arms is necessary – although my Christian faith REQUIRES that I never take part in that activity. I personally would have no choice, along with anyone who claims to follow the Gospel, to be a conscientious objector.

I'm even willing, at this point, to concede certain rifles be permitted for some in the citizenry to hunt and gather food for consumption (not sport). However, non-military personnel should never be permitted to own the same equipment with which the military is armed. The purpose, whether one wishes to engage the subject honestly or not, of the arms that the military bears is singular: to kill other human beings.

I don't believe that anyone, with the begrudging exception granted to military and police personnel, should be permitted to own a handgun, automatic weapon, or anything that was created solely for the execution of other human beings. That is not a right protected by the second amendment and extended to the populace, but a necessary clause to establish and maintain a military force.

In light of this belief and the recent tragedy in Tucson, the horrendous defense of divisive and polarizing rhetoric by some politicians, pundits, and media personalities, and the increasing sense of unrest — particularly on the Internet, I have been trying to understand what this nation's collective obsession with firearms is all about.

The only thing I can surmise is the personal and collective insecurity and inferiority that must be compensated in the alleged need for ownership of these death tools. Fundamentally, I am convinced that the underlying issue is one of control. Guns provide a false sense of power and control for their owners. Knowing that you possess the power to quickly end another person's life, whether you consciously realize this or ever intend to utilize its option, is, I imagine, quite a trip.

There are those who claim, falsely, that they own firearms and carry these weapons on their person in public because these guns provide "safety" or "security." Both of these claims are false. I cannot recall a case (and would be delighted to be told of an instance) in recent history (if ever) when some ordinary citizen carrying or possessing a firearm made a situation "safe" or "secure."

On the contrary, I can think of many instances when children have found firearms and killed themselves or others in play or accidentally, I can think of instances when innocent bystanders have been victims of both intentional and unintentional weapons discharged in public places and, as the former Vice President demonstrated, even the most congenial hunting trips can end in accidental (or not-so-accidental) violence, injury, or death.

I believe that the only explanation for the obsession with firearms in this country — particularly the "bigger," "better," and "deadlier" weapons — has to do with a population that feels very out-of-control. Fear and insecurity plays a big role in all of this, as the renowned academic Abraham Maslow explained in his hierarchy of needs decades ago. The need for security and the feeling of control must be met, and if it isn't met in some constructive, healthy ways, it will be met in less-than-healthy ways like the ardent defense of gun ownership.

As I sat in the Louisville Airport working on this post an older gentleman sat near me. He looked familiar and it wasn't until we were boarding the plane at the same time that I realized it was U.S. Senate Minority Leader, Sen. Mitch McConnell (R-KY) flying back to DC. Having thought through this post and its related ideas, I was eager to speak with him. Unfortunately for me I didn't have the opportunity, but I will say that having two undercover capital police (or secret service, or whatever) with firearms on the tiny regional plane with us did not make me feel safer. Instead, it made me a bit uncomfortable to be that close to such a deadly weapon (times two).

If I had the opportunity to speak with him I would have shared my disappointment with his party's position on the violent and divisive rhetoric that continues to polarize the nation. I would also encourage him and his fellow Republican legislators to change their position on guns in this country. Perhaps we can all work together to make this country a safer land, a more peaceable community so that what we witnessed last weekend might never again happen.

January 13, 2011

23

Catholic Church on Gun Control:
No Firearms for Civilians!

It is indeed fitting that on a weekend marked by the celebration of the life and legacy of Rev. Martin Luther King, Jr. who was assassinated by a firearm, and in the wake of the tragedy in Tucson, Arizona, Catholic News Service (CNS) released a story about the Catholic Church's view on Gun Control.

Bottom line: No guns for civilians. Period.

Finally, some confirmation that your Franciscan Brother here is not off on some planet of his own, but instead finds himself square in-line with what the universal Church teaches.

What makes this fact complicated and likely surprising to so many is that the United States Bishops and other public figures of the Church (and here I include journalists and ecclesial advisors to secular news agencies) have remained quiet on the issue. When the ecclesial leaders of the U.S. Churches and other Catholic documents express concern about small arms and the desire for greater control thereof it generally occurs in passing.

As if to echo precisely what I wrote earlier this week about the need for nation-states to continue to arm themselves, while at the same time striving ever-more ardently for personal/civilian gun restriction, the CNS article states that the Roman Catholic Church's position is described as:

> The Catholic Church recognizes that "states will need to be armed for reason of legitimate defense," as Pope Benedict XVI said in a message to a Vatican-sponsored disarmament conference in April 2008.

> However, armed defense is something appropriate for nations, not for all individual citizens in a state where rule of law is effective, said Di Ruzza.

The CNS article summarizes the Church's stance with the following line: "The answer is resoundingly clear: Firearms in the hands of civilians should be strictly limited and eventually completely eliminated."

For more, you can read the CNS article "Gun Control: Church Firmly, Quietly Opposes Firearms For Civilians."

Perhaps now those Catholics that seem to equate Catholicity with the Republican Party (JFK would be shocked to hear of that, by the way) will call their Representatives and Senators to convince them to increase the limits on civilian gun ownership!

January 16, 2011

24

A Year After Tucson: The Need to Recall Christian Nonviolence

It is hard to believe that it's been a year since the terrible and senseless shooting in Tucson, Arizona, which took the lives of a federal court judge, a 9-year-old girl, and several others, while critically injuring a United States congresswoman — Gabby Giffords — with a gunshot wound to the head. The Pulitzer-Prize winning journalist and my fellow St.

Bonaventure University alum, Dan Barry of the *New York Times* wrote a reflective piece on the anniversary in today's newspaper titled, "A Year Later, 'The Events' Linger." His use of creative quotes to set "The Events" off is reminiscent of one of my favorite, yet hauntingly traumatic euphemisms that is repeated throughout the brilliant Stieg Larsson Millennium books: "when all the evil happened." To describe the horrific moments in life as unspeakable, ineffable encounters with the worst of humanity's freedom can insulate us from a truth of the world in which we live as much as it can serve to gently allow us to express the tragic.

One of the books I received for Christmas and that I've recently read, and by which I was predictably enraptured, was Stanley Hauerwas's new collection of essays *War and the American Difference: Theological Reflections on Violence and National Identity* (Baker 2012). There is so much wisdom that is conveyed in his essays on nonviolence and the role war and violence has played (and continues to play) in the formation and maintenance of United States national identity. I imagine that I will return to this text time and again here at *DatingGod.org* to offer additional reflections, realizing that the insight is so deep and profound, the reflections so manifold, that I cannot capture it all here.

However, there are some things worth considering in light of this one-year anniversary of the tragedy that still haunts many in Arizona, if not throughout the United States — despite the attention-deficit 'news cycle' that quickly moves to the latest fad often at the expense of in-depth and substantial reporting on things, say, like the conditions for the possibility of such an absurd shooting and other forms of inexplicable violence in our world.

Hauerwas states very early on in his new book's introduction:

> My claim [is] that Christians are called to live nonviolently, not because we think nonviolence is a strategy to rid the world of war, but rather because as faithful followers of Christ in a world of war we cannot imagine not living nonviolently...

I think this is an important starting point for Christian

reflections on violence, weapons, and war. It is a non-negotiable stance, one that requires Christians to acknowledge that we should not be able to consider an alternative to nonviolence and at the same time claim a place within the church, which Hauerwas names elsewhere in his introduction as the "alternative politics to the constitutional orders...that are established by war."

Practicality seems to me, in all things uniquely "Christian," to be the gravest of sins. It presents itself under the guise of logic and sensibility, but in fact is an excuse to acquiesce to an order not of Christ's proclamation, nor of the Reign of God announced by the Lord in the Gospels. Instead, in matters related to wealth and evangelical poverty or in matters related to war and violence, the logic of the "world" is taken as the measuring stick against which our actions are to be judged despite our so-called Christian profession.

This is exacerbated by what Hauerwas, and others like James K. A. Smith, calls the liturgical life of nationalism. War becomes sacralized and the sentiments that provide the condition for violence in our culture are ritualized in a way to be celebrated. A case in point is when presidential hopeful and Texas governor Rick Perry stated in last night's republican primary debate that he would "be at the shooting range" on this particular Saturday evening had he not been at the debate (the most common other answer among the candidates was "watching football with the family"). This sort of narrative rhetoric, the elevation of violence (and shooting at paper targets that may or may not contain a silhouette of a human figure *with a machine designed to maim or kill people and animals* is indeed a form of violence) to a place of normalcy such that one would 'naturally' think it normal to fire weapons on a given Saturday evening is frightening.

And we wonder why anyone, young adults or the old alike, finds it strikingly easy to shoot, hurt, and kill strangers?

I will be accused of making leaps in my logic, in transcending the strictures of typical common sense, but I welcome such accusations because, knowledgeable as I am about the ways of the world (and trust me, I am), I aspire to something more. I hope to live a life, as St. Paul exhorts us to do, not by the logic of the world, but by the *ostensibly* impossible wisdom of God. A wisdom that proclaims love for the unlovable, forgiveness for the unforgivable, healing for the broken and brokenhearted.

For although Christian nonviolence seems impossible, if we believe the truth of the messenger to Mary, we should come to realize that "nothing is impossible for God." Perhaps we need to start living that way instead of taking the cowardly and selfish way of the world.

And there is no more relevant a time to reevaluate that aspect of our faith than as we pause to recall the horrors of violence in our world such as what happened a year ago today in Tucson.

When will we learn?

January 8, 2011

25

Death of Bin Laden:
Not a Time to Celebrate, A Franciscan's Prayer for Peace

"As a follower of Jesus Christ, I do not celebrate any human being's violent death. My prayers go out to the entire world tonight. May the fear that has shaped our world in the last decade cease and may peace prevail. No more war. No more violence," my Facebook status reads tonight.

On one hand, this news is something that is being lauded on many fronts. NBC Middle East correspondent Richard Engel congratulated the U.S. Special Forces troops that killed Osama Bin Laden and retrieved his lifeless body. It is news that is being hailed as triumphant and celebratory. And I can understand that. As a citizen of the United States, I can appreciate the ways in which the distorted religious and political views of this deceased man have irrevocably changed the landscape of our society.

Yet, I am a Christian. I cannot take joy, regardless of how much I am tempted to be swept up in the celebratory fervor of my fellow citizens, in the death of my brother in our human family. Yes, Osama Bin Laden committed some horrible, terrible things and led a movement that cannot be supported in any form. Nevertheless, he was a child of God no less than your neighbor, son, daughter, or self.

Let us not forget that in addition to the more-than 3,000 people who have died on September 11, 2001, many thousands more have died since that time here and abroad. More people will also die. And every human death, before its natural end, is a tragedy.

If we proclaim to be "prolife" and value the inherent dignity of every human being from conception to natural death, then we must temper our desire to gloat about the death of one man with the reality that any person's violent and premature death is something to lament. No person's death is an occasion to celebrate.

So, while many — perhaps most — of the United States will be celebrating this news, let all Christians, all Muslims, all Jews, all believers and non-believers — All members of the human family — pause and take this moment as an opportunity to say "never again!"

Never again to violence.

Never again to fear.

Never again to terrorism and the loss of lives in violent death, no matter who those people are.

May all find peace tonight.

May 1, 2011

26

What Does the Bible Say about Bin Laden's Death?

Like so many things, Scripture does not offer us clear responses to contemporary events for the Canon of Scripture is not an answer book, but the historical and religious medium of Divine Revelation. I am grateful to those who have brought these two quotes, one from the Hebrew Wisdom Tradition and the other from the New Testament, both passages considered Holy Scripture for Christians.

Proverbs 24:17-20

Do not rejoice when your enemies fall, and do not let your heart be glad when they stumble, or else the LORD will see it and be displeased, and turn away his anger from them.

Do not fret because of evildoers. Do not envy the wicked; for the evil have no future; the lamp of the wicked will go out.

Matthew 5:43-48

"You have heard that it was said, 'You shall love your neighbor and hate your enemy.' But I say to you, Love your enemies and pray for those who persecute you, so that you may be children of your Father in heaven; for he makes his sun rise on the evil and on the good, and sends rain on the righteous and the unrighteous. For if you love those who love you, what reward do you have? Do not even tax collectors do the same? And if you greet only your brothers and sisters, what more are you doing than others? Do not even the Gentiles do the same? Be perfect, therefore as your heavenly Father is perfect."

As I have already said elsewhere, this is not a moment for "triumph" or "celebration," contrary to what so many television pundits and so-called patriots will suggest. It is indeed an important moment in our national and global history, something to take seriously and reflect upon, but the celebration of the death of a human being is not what Christians are called to do as Jesus makes quite clear above.

God does not desire vengeance and this is not God's form of justice.

It is a sad day, the most recent in many sad days over the course of the last decade. May we take this moment to recommit ourselves to peace and rise up to respond to Jesus's invitation for us to follow in his footprints, living the life of the Gospel. The Gospel of forgiveness and peace, the Gospel of life and humility, the Gospel that calls for the end of all violence.

May 1, 2011

27

Thomas Merton and Christian Nonviolence

Thomas Merton, among his many contributions to Christian spiritual and theological reflection in the last century, had been an outspoken supporter of peace and nonviolence as Christian forms of living in the world. In several essays, Merton identifies nonviolence as not just one option among many, as if there were some choice of personality. As he says in his essay, "Non-Violence and the Christian Conscience," non-violence "is the one political philosophy today which appeals directly to the Gospel." As a way of being-in-the-world, non-violence is richly and overtly Christian.

I have been humbled by the numerous conversations that have been sparked by some of my early reflections on the announcement of the United States assassination of the notorious terrorist Osama Bin Laden. My singular point, expressed in a few different ways over the last twenty-four hours, has been that the death of any member of the human family is never to be the cause of rejoicing, particularly if it is a violent death. Some have implied that, because we believe in the resurrection, every death should be celebrated. Well, I understand that sentiment, but what we really do at something like a funeral mass is celebrate the life, both earthly and the next, of the person who has died — we don't laud death as a good in itself.

I have written elsewhere on the theological and spiritual issues surrounding death (see: "Embracing Sister Death: The Fraternal Worldview of Francis of Assisi as a Source for Christian Eschatological Hope," *The Other Journal* 14), and recognize the place of Christian hope when facing death. Yet, the issue at hand is really one of reaction to violence in our world more than it is to the incidental reality of death. If Bin Laden had died of old age or "natural causes," this would not be so much an issue and I doubt that spontaneous mobs of US Citizens would have gathered in the street chanting jingoistic lines like "USA, USA, USA" or "God Bless America!"

I would like to continue to reflect upon my strongly held belief that to be Christian demands nonviolence. As Merton has also written:

> At a time when so many American Catholics have come to the point where they seem to think that to question the justice of the use of force is to betray the nation and to deny the faith, we need [some] perfectly sound, reasonable and exact argument in favor of Christian non-violence.

> The chief value of such an exposition is that it clearly shows the difference between *non-violence* and *non-resistance*. Not only does non-violence resist evil but, if it is properly practiced, it often resists evil more effectively than violence ever could.

This is an important thing to consider and a truth that has been witnessed globally in the last few months in places like Egypt and Tunisia. Non-violence is a powerful form of resistance and *pacifism* must not be confused with *passivity* as so many mistakenly do. Merton notes, in his essay, "Blessed are the Meek," that a central Scriptural mandate for Christian nonviolence is found in the Sermon on the Mount.

> The chief place in which this new mode of life is set forth in detail is the Sermon on the Mount. At the very beginning of this great inaugural discourse, the Lord numbers the beatitudes, which are the theological foundation of Christian nonviolence: Blessed are the poor in spirit...blessed are the meek (Matt 5:3-4)...

> Furthermore, Christian non-violence and meekness imply a particular understanding of the power of human poverty and powerlessness when they are united with the invisible strength of Christ.

This stems from Merton's discussion of the coming of the

Kingdom of God, as proclaimed by Jesus and which is "realized," he writes, "as Christians themselves live the life of the kingdom in the circumstances of their own place and time."

How is it that we are realizing the Kingdom of God today, in our own places and time? I continue to be challenged to, as the profession of my Franciscan vows begin, "live more perfectly and with firm will The Gospel of Jesus Christ." This means striving to be nonviolent even amid the violence and unrest of our world.

May 3, 2011

28

Franciscan Nonviolence: Called to be Peacemakers

All of this talk in recent days about the ethical or unethical ways to respond to the news of Osama bin Laden's killing has caused me to reflect more and more on what it means to be a *Friar Minor*, a lesser-brother. Particularly, what sort of witness we are to give in the world. As a Franciscan, it is perhaps even more clear that the way in which I and my fellow Franciscan brothers and sisters (friars, poor clares, TOR women and men, and the Secular Franciscans) are to live in the world is in a very clear stance of nonviolent action of peacemaking. There is a centuries-old tradition in each of the branches of the Franciscan family, dating back to the founding of the Orders, that accounts for this disposition and being-in-the-world that is most notably characterized by the total renunciation of violence.

Perhaps the most famous members of the Franciscan family in this regard have been the Secular Franciscans, noted for their compulsory renouncement of arms — even in medieval feudal society — and necessary conscientious objection required by their Rule, which proscribed any use of violence or force. Secular Franciscans have not been allowed, by their profession, to serve in the military (see chapters III and IV of Bob Stewart, OFM's *"De Illis Qui Faciunt*

Penitentiam" The Rule of the Secular Franciscan Order: Origins, Development, Interpretation," [Roma, 1991]).

I have been particularly interested in what the relationship has been and is currently, in explicit terms, between nonviolence and the First Order — that is the Friars Minor. Since I and my brother friars professed to live the Rule and Life of St. Francis *and* the "General Constitutions of the Order of Friars Minor," I thought it might be interesting to see what the current Constitutions say about this matter. What they say is striking and something for all Franciscan friars to note well:

Article 69

(1) In protecting the rights of the oppressed, the friars are to renounce violent action and have recourse to means that are otherwise available even to the powerless.

(2) Conscious also of the terrible dangers that threaten the human race, the friars are to denounce in the strongest terms every kind of warlike action and the arms race as a very serious calamity for the world and a very great injury to the poor; they are to spare neither work nor sacrifice to build up God's kingdom of peace.

Talk about clear and to-the-point! I think there is a tendency, even within the Franciscan community, to look at friars like Fr. Louis Vitale, OFM, and others who protest publicly against the United State's policy of nuclear armament and who, subsequently, are sometimes arrested for civil disobedience, as exceptions to the general rule of daily living of our way of life. Yet, Article 69 of the General Constitutions seems to be clear in its direct command — "the friars are to denounce in the strongest terms every kind of warlike action and the arms race" — that denouncement is to be in the strongest terms.

While there is much more upon which to reflect, and I can assure you that this is something about which I continue to become increasingly more passionate, I thought this passage from the General Constitutions is worth considering during these days. If you are a Franciscan friar, this is very important to recall. If you are not a Franciscan friar, perhaps the example of our way of life — even if many friars struggle sincerely to live it, but fail now and again — may inspire you to do likewise.

Peace and all Good!

May 4, 2011

29

Dear Maureen Dowd:
Yes, We're 'Fools and Knaves' for God

What the Catholic University of America alum and Pulitzer-Prize-winning columnist, Maureen Dowd, seems to have forgotten is that the most popular saint in all of Christian history relished the self-appropriated moniker "God's fool." Francis of Assisi understood himself to be one in stark contrast with the wisdom of the world and the logic of his age. He referred to himself in his own writings as an *idiota* – an idiot, a fool, a clown — for God. His intuition, his desire was to live the life of the Gospel and fulfill his own baptismal promise, which looks very foolish to those who long for the logical, sensical, or "civilized" approach to human and societal interaction. It's a very Pauline approach to the *vita evangelica*.

So, when Maureen Dowd wrote in today's *New York Times* that, "Only fools or knaves would argue that we could fight Al Qaeda's violence non-violently," she was absolutely correct. It is the Christian, Franciscan worldview that believes that one can resist violence with nonviolence.

Has any nation tried that lately? Ever?

Dowd, someone who is occasionally cited in this blog for her insight as well as her caustic tendencies, really misses the mark here. She claims that, "The really insane assumption behind some of the second-guessing is that killing Osama somehow makes us like Osama, as if all killing is the same." From my standpoint, ALL killing is the same. Either *all* life is sacred, or *no* life is sacred. "Thou shalt not kill...unless it's someone like bin Laden," of course! But when or with whom does it stop?

This is not to suggest that we, the 'fools and knaves' for God (which might make a great title for my next book), are against justice — real justice, not vengeance masquerading and called such in a press conference — on the contrary, those who share my Franciscan-Christian outlook believe that justice is certainly called for in the crimes against humanity exhibited in the actions of someone like Osama bin Laden. Yet, violence is not — as Scripture makes clear — the justice that God desires.

Justice would look a lot more like what was proposed by Lawrence Wright in an interview with NPR's Terry Gross on May 2, 2011. Wright suggests that it would have been much more effective if the United States had captured bin Laden alive and taken him to each of the cities in each of the countries where he committed his atrocities to stand trial for each of his horrific crimes. Bin Laden was not just "America's enemy," but a criminal in most of the world.

If Dowd is one thing, she is honest. Her opening lines bespeak her heartfelt response to the news this week, but they also betray her inability to grasp a broader perspective of the situation beyond her own complicity in the seduction of American Nationalism made most apparent in the jingoistic celebration of the news of bin Laden's death.

> I don't want closure. There is no closure after tragedy.

> I want memory, and justice, and revenge.

> When you're dealing with a mass murderer who bragged about incinerating thousands of Americans and planned to kill countless more, that seems like the only civilized and morally sound response.

The NYT columnist goes on to bemoan the theological reflection and moral analysis proffered by writers such as you might find here, calling those efforts "navel gazing."

What a joy-kill I am and those who dare to speak out from amid the congregations of secular liturgies of nationalism and violence that blind its adherents to the Real concealed in the jubilation that "the great 'evil' is dead." All the while Dowd and her compatriots vilify the prophetic voices of Gospel integrity that cry out for a second opinion, that call for a doctor in the audience to assist in a crisis unfolding before our glazed-over eyes.

"Silence!" Dowd and her sympathizers cry. Nobody likes a party-pooper! And, if there is one thing that I am in this moment, it is a proverbial wet blanket. But then again, so have been a lot of people who raise questions about violence in society. Some of those people end up crucified.

Dowd claims that "Morally and operationally, this was counterterrorism at its finest," and she is incorrect. A fine writer she may be, but a moral compass she is not.

Beyond the snarky impulse I have to point out how uncouth it is to end a sentence, let alone a NYT column, with a preposition, I would also like to point out that her columnist coda — "We have nothing to apologize for" — is the saddest thing I have read in some time.

We have much for which to apologize.

Making this world a more violent, unsettled place might be a good start. At least we should offer a collective *mea culpa* for not making this world more peaceable. But then again, Christians — particularly *American* Christians — have never been all that good at pulling those logs out of our own eyes before outing the splinters in eyes of others.

May 7, 2011

30

The Osama bin Laden Assassination Revisited

With the ten-year anniversary of the attacks of September 11, 2001 just a little-more-than a month away, I imagine that there will be a flurry of discussion centered on the death of Osama bin Laden by US Navy SEALS at the beginning of May of the same year. It is hard to imagine that the speeches delivered and the commentaries written next month would not include some reference to the leader of the terrorist organization responsible for the tragedy in 2001. It seems that *The New Yorker* has preempted the anticipated trend with the publication of an article by Nicholas Schmidle titled, "Getting bin Laden: Inside the Raid in Abbottabad." It's fair to say that this is the most detailed depiction of what happened that evening at the beginning of May, it is insightful and thought-provoking to boot.

Having been away on vacation this past week, I was eager to read the article upon my return. I had observed quite a bit of discussion online and elsewhere about this piece and, like so many others, found it well-written and indeed captivating. The revelation of some of the previously unknown details of the plan, raid, and aftermath raised a number of questions for me. Some of these questions compound previously-held concerns, others have spawned from the information presented in this article.

I have not, for the record, changed my position on what I see as yet another tragic chapter in the all-too-long epic that began long before the Tuesday morning in Manhattan ten-years ago. Going back to earlier iterations of colonial and Cold-War interests in Afghanistan and elsewhere, there is historical culpability for what has more recently occurred that has yet to be acknowledged by so many (politicians and ordinary citizens, among others). I continue to maintain that "celebrating" or "rejoicing" in the death of another human being, whether that person is your grandmother or Osama bin Laden, is intrinsically counter to an authentic Christian disposition. It is always and everywhere wrong. The same principles that ground my position in this regard are the same that ground the Christian opposition to things like abortion, capital punishment and war, namely, that *all* human life is sacred and inherently valued. Period.

Nevertheless, such a recognition is often repeated in a misconstrued form that suggests I condone all human *actions*, which is not the case. Bin Laden deserved the be punished and his victims deserved the dignity of justice, but assassination is not justice, it is — ultimately — cowardly and wrong. All killing of human beings is always and everywhere wrong and something to be lamented. Yet, what was done was done and the tide of fervor that sustained joyful (if inebriated and childish) celebration in the streets has passed. Now we are left to recall and evaluate the events and memories of what has come and gone, of what has and will shape the future.

The details presented in *The New Yorker* article confirm that it was not the the mission nor intention of the US Navy SEALS to capture bin Laden and bring him to justice, but to kill him outright.

> A second SEAL stepped into the room and trained the infrared laser of his M4 on bin Laden's chest. The Al Qaeda chief, who was wearing a tan shalwar kameez and a prayer cap on his head, froze; he was unarmed. "There was never any question of detaining or capturing him — it wasn't a split-second decision. No one wanted detainees," the special-operations officer told me.

Yet, there is a parenthetical caveat that the article's author included, one that bears something of an incredulous context in the piece.

> (The Administration maintains that had bin Laden immediately surrendered he could have been taken alive)

From the details present in the article, including the previous dozen sentences or so, it seems that there existed no condition for the possibility of bin Laden's surrender. It was, from the beginning, an assassination mission.

> Nine years, seven months, and twenty days after September 11th, an American was a trigger pull from ending bin Laden's life. The first round, a 5.56mm bullet, struck bin Laden in the chest. As he fell backward, the SEAL fired a second round into his head, just above his left eye. On his radio, he reported, "For God and country — Geronimo, Geronimo, Geronimo." After a pause, he added, "Geronimo E.K.I.A." — "enemy killed in action."

What I found most disturbing about the details of bin Laden's final moments was the report back to the SEAL unit by the sailor who fired the shot: "For God and country." I am 100%

sure that this was not done for God. But that the shooter could think that so readily suggests that this was, in part, the mindset of those tasked with killing the world's #1 most wanted criminal. Surely it was done "for country," of that fact there is no doubt, but what do we make of the claim "For God?"

Likewise, I found, just a few paragraphs later, the much-talked-about mention of Vice President Joe Biden's praying the rosary and comment to Admiral Mullen while viewing the military action puzzling.

> At one point, Biden, who had been fingering a rosary, turned to Mullen, the Joint Chiefs chairman. "We should all go to Mass tonight," he said.

Why? Why did the Catholic Vice President feel as though he and the rest of the group — presumably the Catholic members of the Administration viewing the proceedings of the assassination — go to Mass? Was this a subtle acknowledgement of the complexity of the matter that was both an ostensible "national victory" and a "terrible event?" Was this a desire to pray the *confiteor*, recognizing the complicity in the murder of another human person? Was his comment rooted in a cause for expressing what he recognized as thanksgiving or gratitude for what had just unfolded?

Much of the scuttlebutt has centered on the overly "Catholic" nature of the Vice Presidents behavior and comment — the distinctive Rosary and the desire to go to Mass. But what are we to make of these things? This has been one focus of my reading of the article. Schmidle, the article's author, offered no interpretation or additional context, no response from Mullen, no elements of clarification.

Might these points of consideration, details revealed in the more sober telling of the events of May 2011, provide us with something upon which to reflect as we prepare to mark the ten-year anniversary of the events of September 11th.

August 5, 2011

31

Our Hymn of War and Violence: On the Religion of Nationalism

The course I wrote about the other day, the Honors Seminar in Interreligious Dialogue, at St. Bonaventure University in cooperation with the Chautauqua Institution, has officially entered the Chautauqua phase of the program. Beginning yesterday afternoon and continuing through Saturday afternoon, the students and we professors will participate in the life of Chautauqua. We met our very gracious hosts in the Chautauqua Department of Religion yesterday having officially been welcomed by Maureen Rovegno, assistant director of the department of religion. The first experience our class shared in this Independence-Day Week was the traditional Sacred Song Service on Sunday Night.

The program was titled "O beautiful for patriot dream that sees beyond the years." Organized by Jared Jacobsen, the coordinator of worship and sacred music and organist at Chautauqua, it was a rather stunning experience of narrative, prayer and sacred music.

In his welcome and excellent introductory remarks, Jacobsen explained that he "loved his country very much, but not unequivocally." A statement that resonated with me very well — I knew I was going to like where he was going. He explained that it is always difficult to plan out the worship services near the July 4th Celebration, which is quite impressive at Chautauqua. In a deliberate way, the program had been planned to reflect on those positive things about this particular nation, while acknowledging the painful "historical warts" that we are tempted to far-too-frequently overlook, Jacobsen noted.

The program was very interestingly organized with the bulk of the content focusing on selected narrative passages from Scripture (Isaiah 60), Native American testimony about the "selling" of territories, recollections of the founding of the EPA, the WWII-era internment camps in the US of Japanese and Japanese-Americans, the passing of the PATRIOT Act, the segregation of soldiers, racism, and the praise of the USA's philanthropic efforts around the world. It was, as you can see, rather creatively and starkly composed, seeking to present exactly what Jacobsen introduced was the goal.

It was very telling to see the reaction of the two-thousand or so people who had gathered in the Chautauqua amphitheater for this Sacred Song Service to the final "hymn" of the program, an arrangement of "The Star-Spangled Banner."

There were audience-instructive notes accompanying each portion of the program, and the note that accompanied this piece read: "remain seated."

Yet, before the first note was struck on the organ or the first syllable pronounced by the choir, several people scattered throughout the audience rose to their feet. Their stance, ostensibly chosen as a sign of respect for what they heralded as something "more-than a musical piece," caused a number of our group — myself included — to critically consider what was happening here.

I've said for years that those theorists, scholars of religion, philosophers, and theologians who talk about the Religion of Nationalism and study "Secular Liturgies" (a term borrowed from James K. A. Smith), are correct in their assessments of the United States and its population. Can a nation-state stand to exist without an official, or in this case unofficial, "State Religion?"

While the constitution of the United States grants the right for all citizens and residents to practice the private religion of their choice, while legally guaranteeing the state's refusal to endorse any singular tradition, there is something else very curiously happening over the 200+ year history of this country. The seeming religious vacuum of "State Religion" has been replaced by "Nationalism," in which rituals, creedal claims, and the demarcating of spaces, times, people and places as "Sacred" and "profane" exist as in most other religious traditions.

The choice to stand during the playing of this song in

direct opposition to the instruction of the program, thereby setting oneself apart from the crowd, may have seemed to the individuals as the "right thing to do," thanks to years of indoctrinating (note the root "doctrine") formation from kindergarten through military service to cultural and political cues that exist in subtle, daily ways.

Yet, to several students and certainly to these professors of theology and religion, what was seen as protest-rooted-in-some-form-of-patriotism to the actors, was also interpreted as religious zealotry. It is not unlike those protestors in worship services that take into their own hands the liturgical, theological, and expressive liberties that lead, for example, to congregants standing/kneeling/sitting when the rest of the worship assembly is reverently and unitedly participating according to custom and tradition. As a Roman Catholic religious and priest, I see this happening most often in my tradition when people drop to their knees during portions of the Eucharistic Liturgy because of their own personal sense of what is and is not sacred and appropriate. It is a form of religious affectivity and zealotry, innocuous perhaps on one hand, but significant no less. These sorts of things happen in every other religious tradition as well.

What leads to this sort of behavior? In order for someone to go against the grain of a community's set form of decorum and behavior, a person must be seriously convicted. From their own perspective, a religious conviction of a significant order must compel them to make a public protest that self-identifies such a person as exceptionally devotional or pious standing when one is supposed to sit or kneeling when one is supposed to stand.

Those who stood, if asked (and I partly wished I had time to speak with some of these folks, although more opportunities are sure to arise in the coming days), might likely say that, "this is what one does" or identify the instructed behavior as "disrespectful." But what or whom is not being respected? This is what got me thinking about the United States National Anthem and what a song of that sort really means. First of all, it only became the national anthem in the 1930s, which by itself means little, except to point out that this ancient sense of the sacred and the perennial references to the

68

"founding fathers" evoked in such instances of religious nationalism is entirely contrived.

Secondly, and most importantly, the context and content of the poem written by Francis Scott Key in 1814 about the battle of Fort McHenry in the War of 1812 and set to the tune "To Anacreon in Heaven," is a poem about war and violence. Unlike the predecessor to "The Star Spangled-Banner," the *de facto* pre-1931 "national anthem," "My Country 'Tis of Thee," there is little celebratory and positive content to the current anthem. Although it was written as something of a satirical protest of "God Save the Queen," "My Country 'Tis of Thee," is not written about war nor does it bear the hints of the manifest destiny and justified violence latently present in "The Star-Spangled Banner."

What does it mean that the symbols and hymns of the public and secular religion of "American" Nationalism are rooted in violence and war? That people would in protest and disrespect stand to reverence such things? That women and men talk about dying for country, but would not risk the discomfort of the demands called for by their Christian (or other religious) faith?

There is much for us to think about as we prepare for what I like to call "the Easter of American Nationalism," the celebration of July 4th. Look around on the 4th, do you recognize the saturation of religious imagery and symbolism? There is much more going on that we should consider and upon which to reflect.

July 2, 2012

PART 3

DIFFICULT SITUATIONS
AND CHALLENGES IN THE CHURCH

32

Why I Do Not Support the (so-called) March for Life

There are indeed numerous reasons to withhold support for the so-called "March for Life." I wish here to highlight three of the reasons I have serious reservations about the annual 'pilgrimage' to Washington, DC, that draws thousands of well-meaning people, the young and the old alike. Ah, but before I go further, I feel as though I need to qualify that last sentence. While the generational divide is usually traversed by a diverse representation of different ages and from idealistic youth and young adults to the more narrowly focused and opinion-concretized geriatric crowd, there is very little racial and ethnic diversity represented. Anticipating the likely unhappy responses in what will appear in the comment section below, I suppose it is necessary to acknowledge that there are indeed African-American, Latino/a, and Asian women and men who arrive for the events of the annual pilgrimage. However, their numbers reflect that category into which they are so blindly corralled in this country – a minority. The sea of protesters (and that is what they are, protesters) is overwhelmingly white and that is not an insignificant dimension of the event.

Among the various reasons one might chose to omit him or herself from participation, I wish to highlight three: (a) the event's moniker is incomplete at best and disingenuous at worst; (b) the mode of protest has proven ineffective; and, following the second point, (c) the 'march' and its related events are a self-serving exercise in self-righteousness, self-congratulatory grandstanding; and disinterest in the most pressing matters of human rights and dignity in our world today.

To begin, I have no problem with people of faith taking a public stance against abortion. You will never find me supporting abortion legislation nor encouraging those with and for whom I minister as a Roman Catholic cleric to support abortion. I believe it is a legitimate issue against which, as a Christian and Roman Catholic, I feel should be a thematic feature of social transformation. However, it is not, at all, *the most important issue,* nor is it the single issue upon which Catholics – or anyone – should focus their attention s in an exclusive manner.

Abortion belongs to a series of social sins of a systemic degree that include capital punishment, war and violence, limitation of social services for the least among us, economic inequality, abject poverty, and other threats to the dignity of human persons in our culture and globalized world. Some will claim that abortion is more egregious than those other things because of the so-called innocence of the fetuses whose life is prematurely ended. Yet, innocence is a construct that has theological and ethical implications and characteristics that have been explored on this website as well as on the excellent *WIT: Women in Theology* website. I will not rehearse those discussions here.

Instead, what is necessary is to recognize the shortcomings of what is too often uncritically lauded among certain sectors of the Catholic and more broad Christian communities as the "pro-life" event *par excellence.* In fact, it is a striking show of support for anti-abortion protests, but offers little (with very few, and always marginal, exceptions) by way of a truly Catholic (and catholic, as in universal)[†] pro-life demonstration. Such an event would include a much broader representation of the issues that also threaten life and human dignity.

And so I offer this rather non-exhaustive reflection on three points I think need to be considered with regard to assessing the (so-called) "March for Life" each January in Washington, DC.

A. The Disingenuousness of its Title

While those who trek to the nation's capital to stand in the chilly January air are undoubtedly sincere in their

---

[†] The use of "catholic" here is the colloquial English usage sense denoting "universal," but for more on the meaning and origin of the word "catholic," see Daniel Horan, "'Catholic' Doesn't Mean What You Think it Does," *The Huffington Post* (October 20, 2012) available at www.HuffingtonPost.com

conviction, I wonder about the provenance of the march and its title. The march is presented as a positive effort (hence the preposition "for"), yet it really is a protest *against* something. Ostensibly, it is a protest *against* a United States Supreme Court ruling thirty-nine years ago that grants women the right to procure safe, regulated, and legal medical abortions.

To claim that the march's focus has anything to do with other matters of justice, human dignity, or social justice is contradicted by the endless parade of ecclesiastical and civil politicians that speak at the Vigil Mass the night before and then at the march itself. The focus is very clear: *Roe vs. Wade* and its overturning.

I might be more apt to support an anti-abortion rally or march *against* the *Roe vs. Wade* decision if such an event was given its proper title and promotion. Instead, moral agency is replaced by pre-emptive and divisive rhetorical deployment in the way that those who gather in the streets of the District of Columbia bearing placards featuring inhumane depictions of aborted fetuses and other such means of attention-seeking present themselves as the "good" (they are, of course, "*for* life"), and anyone who does not march alongside them, joining the rabble of discontented churchgoers, is therefore "bad."

In other words, someone such as myself, an honest and outspoken critic of this particular event, is cast as "bad" or "pro-abortion" by way of omission and my particular absence from the group. Likewise, anyone who finds the means by which this organized and self-congratulatory annual event questionable or disingenuous, those who chose not to partake in the happenings of the march, are similarly considered – if tacitly – "bad."

Call me what you will, but I'll call the march what it is: an "anti-abortion rally" under the guise of a "pro-life event."

B. Lack of Desired Effect and Absence of Purpose

I am the first to argue the one's ethical *telos* shouldn't always be "success" or "accomplishment" according to the standards of the world (in line with the Pauline epistolary). In the case of nonviolence, for example, "success" is often cited as the most justified reason for war and military action. Pacifists will argue that such an end – "success" – is not a category that Christians should appropriate. However, when someone does claim a specific goal as the desired end of an effort, then I think it is fair to evaluate one's actions based on that aim.

When asked what they want, why they gather, and why they march, those assembled today for the "March for Life" will readily reply: "to overturn *Roe vs. Wade*," by which they mean: "to make abortion illegal in the United States."

For nearly forty years people have been doing *the exact same thing* with no progress of which to speak. That classic definition of insanity comes to mind: doing the same thing over and over again, while expecting a different result. It would appear clear that the method currently in anti-abortion-protest-vogue is not working. If anything the number of abortions have increased in the US (most notably and strikingly during the previously esteemed "champion" of the pro-life movement, President George W. Bush). And yes they continue to persist under a Democratic presidential administration too.

Which sheds light on my point: what is the purpose of this march? Is it a political rally? Is it a Republican effort? Is it a Democratic effort? Or, is it a Religious effort? If it is the latter, then perhaps some serious prayer and discernment is needed so that something can be done in an effort to effect the goal desired by those well-meaning women and men who take time away from families and jobs to march around the streets of DC and sight-see at the Basilica and National Mall.

I don't care for events that do not have any chance of effecting the goal set out for the effort.

Try something new if you are *really* serious about reducing or ending abortions.

Perhaps caring for young adults who become pregnant, taking care of unwed mothers, offering good school systems for the children who are carried to term and brought into this world – all of these would be good places to begin.

Perhaps those, mostly white, marchers would do well to consider the racial, gender, ethnic, socio-cultural, and economic issues that undergird the abortion questions in this country. It is never, *never* as simple as "good" versus "bad," "pro-life" versus "pro-death," and so on.

Perhaps I would be more sympathetic to the movement to parade through the streets of Washington, DC, in protest of a forty-year-old Supreme Court decision if I was more convinced of the sincerity of the protesters to do what it is they claim they want, which, if they are truly Christians, demands so very much more of them than getting on a bus for a two-day road trip each January.

C. An Exercise in Self-Congratulatory Fanfare

This leads me to my final reservation of this post, a point of reflection on which I will conclude these thoughts. While the presenting focus of the "March for Life" is the abortion legislation of the United States, what actually takes place seems far less issue-focused and far more an exercise in self-congratulatory fanfare.

I have heard numerous people, even those who avidly support the march, lament that the Vigil Mass has become more a "Who's Who" of a sector of the American Catholic Church than it has the Eucharistic celebration it alleges to be. What amounts to a veritable "party convention," with its requisite and seemingly endless congratulatory introductions and "thank yous" to all the US churchmen, the event takes on a sense of the spectacle over and against the sense of the sacred it might otherwise elicit.

What strikes me as most egregious in this whole extravaganza is the simplistic distillation of an incredibly complex moral and political issue into the binary "good vs. evil" construction. It is not that simple. Furthermore, as stated above, anything in the Catholic tradition that claims to be "pro-life" – person or event – must also include those other important issues of life and dignity, issues that most of these marchers would otherwise prefer to forget: war, poverty, torture, capital punishment, economic inequality, and the like.

It is sad that a boutique, albeit legitimate, issue in the Catholic moral tradition has been made to be the singular and defining catholicity litmus test for so many. Who is in and who is out is rarely determined by one's profession of faith and baptism (that is, by the way, what makes someone a Christian), but where they fall in the pseudo-reality of binary moral categories: "pro-life or not?" which always really means: "anti-abortion" – if only nominally, because no one marching who knows anything about the political system in the US actually thinks a president or a congressman or a supreme court justice can overturn such a contentious and constitutionally protected law – "or not?"

I look forward to the day when we do assemble thousands of young people and old people alike to march through the streets of the nation's capital in order to support a movement *for life* and *for human dignity*. But until the annual January event *really* addresses the matter of what it means to be *for life* (literally, "pro-life"), I cannot support it.

I will pray though, as I often do, for all those issues of life and human dignity that get left by the roadside as the marchers in DC parade to the Capitol, their Jerusalem. Perhaps, just maybe, a single Samaritan or even a few might be among the crowd and stop to pick up the ignored and forgotten and left-for-dead issues that continue to threaten life and human dignity in our world.

January 23, 2012

33

Race, Poverty, and the Voice of Power: A Response to "March for Life"

I left for work yesterday morning to record the audio version of my book (*Dating God: Live and Love in the Way of St. Francis*) at the studios of St. Anthony Messenger Press in Cincinnati having only glanced at the handful of comments on the blog. At the time, rather early in the morning, only a few hundred people had visited the post and I was able to engage in some conversation among the commenters. When I returned last evening thousands had visited the post and an article on the front page of *The National Catholic Reporter* website lauded the piece for the "calm and reason" of the post as well as the seeming civility of the subsequent commenters. That has, of course, been challenged by a handful of rather caustically defensive comments that at-times verge on the inappropriate. Why all this anger?

My guess is that what I shared by way of my reflections — and, to the commenter who thought otherwise, that rather lengthy blog post was never, nor never would be, a "homily" — touched on some all-too-infrequently discussed truths about an annual event that is nearly universally celebrated by a particular segment of the American Catholic Church. It is never easy to be "called out" on unfavorable characteristics, yet the true character of a person is revealed in how he or she responds to such consideration. It would seem that some handled it well, but many did not.

Before I offer a response to an issue that I did not have much of an opportunity to address yesterday, mentioning the composition of the protesting demographics only in passing, I want to be clear about a few things lest there remains any confusion. The post yesterday was simply my expression of *why I do not support* the annual march in Washington, DC. Some commenters — here, on Facebook and elsewhere — seem to think that I was making a case to attack those who gather for those events. Not at all. I was sharing why *I will not* participate. It is a valid and necessary move to highlight why a well educated, Roman Catholic cleric of a Religious Order, who resides just outside DC, would not participate nor support the "March for Life."

If the reflection caused you to pause and feel as though you were being attacked, I suggest you explore those feelings to find their source. Is there something in that post that speaks to your experience that you have not before noticed or would otherwise prefer to ignore? I surmise that the feelings of defensive resentment that arose in response to my expression of lack-of-support for this event come from a place of conscience that acknowledges what has been said resonates with one's experience, but pride or the desire to proceed with impunity and righteousness clouds the ability for one to accept the critique.

So, to the heart of today's post: *Who are the most vulnerable among us?*

This question lies at the heart of my naming a truth that several commenters found very irritable yesterday. I mentioned that, despite some various exceptions, the composition of the protesting, anti-abortion crowds are mostly white women and men. The issue of race is indeed a sensitive one and one about which I am hardly qualified to address in any authoritative way. However, I am very aware of my social location and its relationship to the issues, culture and church around me.

For instance, I struggle with the real tension that exists in the United States (or more generally, "The West") between the dual and at-times contradictory identities I inhabit as (a) a Franciscan Friar, which means "Lesser Brother," and (b) a white, male, highly educated, Roman Catholic Cleric of middle-class origins who is a United States citizen.

See, for Francis of Assisi — and our Rule or way of life makes this clear — the social location that the Friars are to inhabit is one of marginal status, in solidarity with what we might today call those of the subaltern experience in our world. Friars, precisely as Lesser Brothers, define themselves in contradistinction with places and positions of power and all of these considerations, in addition to others, makes my experience a challenging one to negotiate today.

How does a "white, male, highly educated, Roman Catholic cleric of middle-class origins who is a United States citizen" live as a "Lesser Brother" (Friar Minor) today?

It is with that sensitivity to social location, gender, race, class and power that I view the events that unfold each January in Washington, DC, as literal busloads of well-meaning people pour into the nation's capital for two days of protest, socialization and tourism.

I raised the question of the racial composition of the crowds precisely to call attention to the fact that in seeking to name an injustice in our society — ostensibly, the goal of the protest/march is to draw attention to the injustice of abortion — those who are most vulnerable in our society remain, yet again, unrepresented and silenced.

So that I cannot be accused of lacking empirical evidence, I suggest you check out *The Washington Post* photo gallery from yesterday's March-related events. Look very closely at each image. What do you see? It looks a lot like I anticipated at 5:00 am yesterday morning from a friary in Cincinnati as I published that blog post: young and old white people. What does this mean? Perhaps nothing. But it might also mean that there are question we must raise about *who is speaking* and *for whom?*

The category of class is usually much more difficult to identify by sight. Yet, if my hunch about the racial composition of the crowd of the March was correct, I might take my chances to surmise that most of those protesters were solidly middle class or upper middle class white people, most of whom attend private secondary schools of education and many who are college-educated or being college-educated.

These people do not represent the voice of the most vulnerable of our society. Theirs is the voice of power.

Now, those in social locations of privilege and power (which is where white middle-class US citizens are, especially men — just read Peggy McIntosh's classic essay "White privilege: Unpacking the Invisible Knapsack" if you don't already recognize this) should have a say in the public square and have a right to express themselves as they do on days like yesterday.

My concern, however, is for *those who do not have a voice*. Do not mistake my concern for an excuse not to express myself, but rather it is a concern that leads me to raise questions about what is actually happening at an event like the "March for Life" instead of merely and uncritically accepting what people *claim* is happening at such an event.

Does diversity in race, class and gender necessarily make such an event legitimate? Am I claiming that the "March for Life" is therefore not legitimate because of its blatantly exclusive composition of participants? No and No.

What *I am saying* is that you cannot just take things at face value, that this particular issue seems to appeal almost exclusively to white people of privilege and power says something. It says to me that embracing a movement that claims to speak on behalf of the "most vulnerable" in our society in fact stands without the voice of the very same people. I dare say that one of the dangers of the "March for Life" is that it becomes an opportunity, perhaps a catharsis, each year for people of racial, gender and class privilege to sublimate their intuitive instinct for justice on an issue and in a manner that proves safe and yet ineffective.

Meanwhile, who hears the voices of the most vulnerable children of color and poverty in South East DC, struggling in some of the worst neighborhoods, schools and social matrices in the country? As the privileged white, privately educated young women and men of the country march down the streets of the capital for the unborn, who is marching for the post-born? There are clearly thousands of people of a particular social location in this country who will give up two days of school and work for victims of abortion, but who will do the same for the victims of economic inequality, violence, war, unjust prison systems and the like?

Whether you like it or not, race, class and power play into these things much more significantly than one might at first realize. That is my point.

January 24, 2012

34

Can You Be "Pro-Life" and "Pro-Death penalty?"

The Washington Post has raised precisely this question following GOP presidential hopeful Rick Perry's response to a debate question last week during which Perry was asked about his record on the death penalty. The Post explains: "During a GOP debate last week, Texas Governor Rick Perry was asked about his support of the death penalty. (Texas has the highest rate of execution in the country.) Rick Perry was steadfast, saying, to cheers of support from the audience, that he had "never struggled" with the potential that Texas could have execution of an innocent person. At a June 2011 anti-abortion event, Perry told supporters that he believes "human life [is] a sacred gift from God." Can you be pro-life and pro-death penalty? How does one reconcile these positions?"

What followed was a multi-voice conversation that included opinions from five authors. The authors varied in their response to the question about whether one can appropriate the moniker "Pro-Life" while maintaining a position that supports the continued execution of prisoners.

The author that most closely represents my position on this matter is Susan Brooks Thistlethwaite, whose piece is titled, "Who would Jesus Execute?" She makes the convincing, if quick, argument that what is represented by people like Perry and the crowd that twice cheered the Texas Governor's infamous reputation for executing criminals is more in line with Ancient Roman (i.e., quite literally, "pagan") theology than the theology of Christianity.

Thistlehwaite makes the interesting point, drawing on the well-known scripture scholar, John Dominic Crossan's work, that what is really at the heart of this divide — Roman vs. Christian worldview — is *power*. This should not come as a surprise to any of us who understand the power dynamics at play when Christianity is appropriated for partisan polity (in any circumstance, not simply by the GOP in this instance). She explains:

> Romans were all about using power to control people; Jesus, by contrast, was about power shared in his program of "heal the sick, eat with those you heal, and announce the Kingdom's presence in that mutuality." The New Testament presents us with a struggle between two different kinds of power, Crossan argues, the Roman imperial model of power that promises "peace through victory," victory guaranteed by lethal force, or "Jesus's peace through justice."

She makes the claim that, "much of the 'pro-life' position seems to come from a similar view of power; it's all about control, a top down conception of power." She notes that the consistent ethic of life approach, made well-known by the late Cardinal Bernardin of Chicago, seeks to offer a holistic approach to this ostensible disconnect among Christians who claim to be "Pro-Life," yet support politicians and policies that continue to threaten human dignity and the sanctity of life, such as the death penalty.

Some of the other authors offer contrasting perspectives,

arguing at times in favor of the death penalty and the ability of a Christian to claim pro-life status while supporting state-sponsored executions. The pro-death penalty scriptural mainstay is Romans 13, which, in part, reads: "God's servant, an agent of wrath to bring punishment on the wrongdoer" (Rom. 13:4). Yet, the renown moral theologian Stanley Hauerwas of Duke University (named by TIME magazine in 2001 as "America's Best Theologian") has consistently said that you cannot read Romans 13 outside the context established by its previous chapter Romans 12. That preceding section sets a very different tone for the passage invoked by pro-death penalty people than its out-of-context or proof-texting citation allots.

September 15, 2011

35

I Will Also Not Leave the Church

Often the source of some controversy himself, E.J. Dionne, the Catholic columnist for the *Washington Post*, whose syndicated columns get a lot of attention, has called out a rather controversial organization that is taking the current crises within (and without) the Roman Catholic Church as an opportunity to encourage folks to leave the Church. Like, Dionne, I am not going anywhere!

Dionne explains the impetus for his reflections in a column titled, "I'm Not Quitting the Catholic Church."

> Recently, a group called the Freedom from Religion Foundation ran a full-page ad in The Washington Post cast as an "open letter to 'liberal' and 'nominal' Catholics." Its headline commanded: "It's Time to Quit the Catholic Church."

> The ad included the usual criticism of Catholicism, but I was most struck by this paragraph: "If you think you can change the church from within — get it to lighten up on birth control, gay rights, marriage

equality, embryonic stem-cell research — you're deluding yourself. By remaining a 'good Catholic,' you are doing 'bad' to women's rights. You are an enabler. And it's got to stop."

My, my. Putting aside the group's love for unnecessary quotation marks, it was shocking to learn that I'm an "enabler" doing "bad" to women's rights. But Catholic liberals get used to these kinds of things. Secularists, who never liked Catholicism in the first place, want us to leave the church, but so do Catholic conservatives who want the church all to themselves.

E. J. Dionne is correct, about the myopic and partisan lens this organization has with regard to seeing the Roman Catholic Church. It is, as we loyal Catholics recognize (noting that loyalty, love and relationship all denote the occasional need for a charitable challenge), a human organization. One guided by the Holy Spirit, but a fallible, finite, human organization no less.

Yet, despite the weaknesses of the members of the Church — including, and especially, its leaders — that business about the Holy Spirit is the biggest reason that we continue to stay. Or, as Dionne puts it: "They may not see the Gospel as a liberating document, but I do, and I can't ignore the good done in the name of Christ by the sisters, priests, brothers and lay people who have devoted their lives to the poor and the marginalized." It is in living out Matthew 25 that the Church best exhibits the work of the Spirit in the world. True, it may not always be easy to see, it may not appear in a *New York Times* article, but it is happening all over the world everyday.

Dionne is also correct about a certain faction in the Church that wishes it had the institutional structure all to itself. These are those who advocate a so-called "leaner, smaller, purer" church, those who forget that Jesus called the weak, voiceless, ordinary and sinful to follow him, not the moral elite or the ecclesiastical leadership of his day.

In his column, Dionne praises Pope John XXIII and Pope John Paul II for their social-justice efforts. But he also challenges the current bishops in some important ways:

> I'd like the FFRF to learn more about the good Pope John, but I wish our current bishops would think more about him, too. I wonder if the bishops realize how some in their ranks have strengthened the hands of the church's adversaries (and disheartened many of the faithful) with public statements — including that odious comparison of President Obama to Hitler by a Peoria prelate last month — that threaten to shrink the church into a narrow, conservative sect.

> Do the bishops notice how often those of us who regularly defend the church turn to the work of the nuns on behalf of charity and justice to prove Catholicism's detractors wrong? Why in the world would the Vatican, apparently pushed by right-wing American bishops, think it was a good idea to condemn the Leadership Conference of Women Religious, the main organization of nuns in the United States?

Some will read Dionne's remarks (and I suppose my reposting of them here) as an "action against the bishops," but such people must realize that silence and "blind faith" is not what it means to be a Christian. We are called, as the two-millennia-old theological tradition of the Church reminds us, to use our *reason* in "faith seeking understanding." Sometimes tough love is necessary to express the sincerity with which we embrace the faith, and challenging questions are a good example of such love. As Dionne alludes, if we didn't love the Church, we'd simply leave like the others have.

Pointing again to Pope John XXIII's writing, Dionne's final paragraphs hit the nail on the head.

> Too many bishops seem in the grip of dark suspicions that our culture is moving at breakneck speed toward a demonic end. Pope John XXIII, by contrast, was more optimistic about the signs of the times.

> "Distrustful souls see only darkness burdening the

face of the earth," he once said. "We prefer instead to reaffirm all our confidence in our Savior who has not abandoned the world which he redeemed." The church best answers its critics when it remembers that its mission is to preach hope, not fear.

May we live as people of hope, preaching with our actions and words the *Good News* of Jesus Christ, not the fear the world already gives.

May 14, 2012

36

What the Church Can Learn from Egypt: A Short Treatise

Youth, Social Media, Respect and Dialogue.

These are four of the themes, lessons perhaps, that I feel can be gleaned by the Church from events of the past few weeks and need to be taken seriously today. There are certainly many more characteristics that legitimately offer foci upon which we should reflect as a pilgrim church, but here are just a few points that have struck me as timely and relevant for our communal consideration.

The Need to Recognize the Place of Young Adults

One thing that has struck so many around the world as a fascinating dimension of the popular revolution in Egypt has been the youthfulness of the movement. Egypt is a largely young country, PBS's *Newshour* reported last Friday that half of the Egyptian population is under the age of 25. While many so-called "Western" nations (The U.S., Canada, many members of the European Union, for example) are suffering from a declining population, much of the global population remains young.

Additionally, the Church has suffered by way of Church attendance and sacramental participation in many Western nations, while the Church continues to grow and blossom in those parts of the world that reflect a much more youthful constitution.

The Church, particularly those in leadership positions within the community, would be wise to take note of the power of young adults. The youth bear, s not authoritarian power, but a transformative power that is both charismatic and inspirational. Their optimism — commonly dismissed by this generation's cynical predecessors, as was the case in the so-called Arab World until last week — is a force for positive change, renewal and prophetic challenge.

Today's youth are not the "future church" about which septua- and octogenerian prelates and lay ministers so often speak of these days. The youth *are the Church,* for the Church is the entire Body of Christ with all its members — young and old alike. Take young adults very seriously and welcome their enthusiasm, hopefulness and optimism as signs of the Holy Spirit's continued work in our world and Church. Listen to them!

The Need to Use Social Media

In addition to the youthfulness of the movement, something that has captured the attention of much of the world is the communication and organization that was made possible through the engagement with social media technology like Facebook and Twitter. Were these media the *cause* of revolution? Certainly not, but they were the condition for the possibility of mobilization and the sharing of information otherwise made impossible.

Both the Pope and the United States Bishops have, within the last few months, independently released statements and spoken about the need — really the obligation — the Church has, particularly for its leaders, to use these new media in reaching out to the world.

As I've said elsewhere, Facebook and Twitter, Blogs and electronic publications are not the exclusive or fleeting domain of the young, but the latest in communications innovation that will not disappear — just as the Internet, television, telephone, and printing press have not disappeared previously. While the media will continue to change and develop, it's not going away. And to be where the people are means to be engaged with these forms of communication.

The whole Church's use of this technology is not an end in itself, but a means for which our engagement is imperative, not optional!

The Need for Respect Among All

Beyond the youthfulness and social-media-use that has captured the attention of so many, the respectful and non-violent action of the movement in Egypt (and, now, many surrounding nations in the so-called Arab World) has become iconic and inspirational.

Forceful, direct, and deliberate may be fine qualifiers for the demonstrations and demands expressed by the people, but respectful and peaceful may also be counted among the descriptors. There was no war, there was no violence (on the part of demonstrators prior to isolated and provoked incidences), and there was a sense of solidarity and respect that arose from the resistance to injustice.

The Church has a lot to learn from this movement in this regard. All voices must be heard and respected. Being as involved in social media as I am, I see daily disrespectful comments that root themselves in rude caricatures and *ad hominem* attacks — all in the "defense of the Church" (or "faith," or whatever). This is not what we are about as Christians, this is not what we should be about as human beings and citizens of a global community.

All must be respected, all voices heard, and non-violence — in action and speech — must be the collective *modus operandi* of the leaders and all in the Church!

The Need for Honest and Open Dialogue

Finally, there is a need for dialogue in the Church. This is something made very timely by the German-speaking theologians who have recently published an open letter to the Bishops of those nations, raising legitimate concerns — rooted in sound theological scholarship — about certain matters of governance and disciplinary traditions in the Church.

The call for dialogue is absolutely essential. Theology is, as St. Anselm famously coined, "faith *seeking understanding*." Orthodoxy is *not* about "Blind Faith" or repetitious defense of this or that articulation. Our faith is living, our Creeds and Scriptures continue to speak to us and the Spirit continues to inspire. We are called to better understand what we believe, and therefore better understand God and ourselves, through the engagement of our faith in a sincere effort to understand it.

This is not to suggest that every recommendation or request can necessarily take root. As systematic theologians often say, our Scripture and Tradition are both elaborative *and* descriptive. There are limits to what we can say about the faith with regard to doctrinal matters — we can't really talk about whether or not Christ is Divine or whether or not God is Triune. Those matters are set, yet their understanding, what those statements *mean*, need to be further clarified.

At the same time, issues that are not doctrinal or dogmatic, disciplinary matters like clerical celibacy or who may be ordained to ministry should be on the table for discussion. How else can we better understand our faith if we don't actually seek that understanding through preclusion, regardless of the outcome?

I get the impression at times that people who react strongly against open dialogue really do not believe in the Holy Spirit or the Faith, including certain prelates. If you believe in the Spirit's guidance of the Church, God's continued working in the world, then what is there to fear?

Heresy has long been overcome historically, the first seven ecumenical councils of the Church are great examples of this — most bishops walked in with a popular, and later termed heretical, understanding of a given statement of faith, only to be inspired otherwise. Let the dialogue ensue, trust in God and the Holy Spirit. To those who recoil at this invitation, I respond "ye, of little faith!"

There is much more that can be said on these subjects and I welcome your continued dialogue and conversation in a spirit, of course, of respect and openness. What has transpired in the last three weeks around the world should not be lost on any citizen of this age, nor should it be overlooked by the Church, which is the Body of Christ.

February 15, 2011

37

RCIA and the Responsibility of Our Faith Community

Rather randomly, I read a guest piece in the *Washington Post* written by a man in Maryland named Bob Arscott describing his experience of conversion to the Roman Catholic Church. The piece, titled "Converting to Catholicism a Challenging but Rewarding Decision," stood in stark contrast to a few other stories about Catholicism that I read this morning in my attempt to 'catch up' on some news, particularly of a religious theme, while I'm on the road visiting family and friends for the holidays (which, by the way, will explain the more intermittent postings here for the past few and the next few days).

I was rather touched by his direct and, frankly, positive reflection on the experience and his own spiritual journey that led him to make this decision to enter into full communion (the technical term) with the Roman Church. Far too often the focus, by way of media or simple word-of-mouth, is of the numbers of people who *leave* the Church. Those who, oftentimes for very understandable reasons, have been hurt or pushed out by their Church, then decide to make a more definitive break with the community.

Yet, here was a man, who by his own recollection had a very healthy and normal life.

> When I entered into the Rite of Christian Initiation of Adults program, I did so with an open mind. Every Sunday, my enthusiasm increased. I wanted to discover more about Catholicism. But there were also times I had doubts. There were times when others in class talked of the tragedies in their lives

that drew them to the Catholic faith. But I felt my life was normal. My family was healthy.

Why was he doing this? he asks. What was drawing him to the RCIA (Rite of Christian Initiation of Adults) program and the Church?

His answer is touching: " I came to realize God had been looking after me my entire life. My skills that had seen me through difficult and dangerous situations were a gift from God and there is no such thing as luck, just divine intervention."

He goes on to explain that, "During the months I spent preparing to become Catholic, I learned about the faith, the significance of the Mass, how to live my life by the Church's teachings, how to pray, and how to live in a community of Christians."

What a positive reflection of the purpose of RCIA. Indeed, the last note of his description sums it all up: *how to live in a community of Christians!*

This is what *all* Christians, Catholics and others included, should strive to learn throughout our spiritual journeys. The so-called "cradle catholics" (myself included) sometimes take our faith and church for granted and do not appreciate the richness of our tradition, the depth of our faith and the connection to one another and Christ that is formed by our baptism.

Bob Arscott's reflection really inspired me today to pray for those who are in the process of the RCIA and for those who help facilitate that program around the world. As one of my former liturgy professors liked to emphasize and re-emphasize often, the RCIA program is the model for the whole faith community's catechesis! We are all on spiritual journeys that require deepening our faith, learning how to pray, being reconnected to the community and sharing our stories.

The RCIA process is perhaps one of the best things our Church does, let's not take it for granted. To facilitate that program well is the responsibility of our entire faith community, not just one or two well-meaning people. May the remaining days of the octave and season of Christmas be a time for us to pause and recall what it means for us to grow in our faith and to help others do the same.

December 29, 2011

38

Listening to the Church of Today: Youth and Young Adults

It's interesting that the *Catholic News Service* article that reports Pope Benedict XVI's arrival to Spain ran with the title: "Pope says Listening To, Praying With Young Is a Great Joy." It's interesting because I find the claim that many leaders in the Church like to (or actually) listen to today's young adults difficult to believe. Not because I wish to challenge the sincerity with which such claims are made, but because I have a hard time finding examples of this in practice. The article reports:

> World Youth Day, [the Pope] said, reminds them that they are not alone in their journey with God and gives them an opportunity to share their hopes, their cultures and "motivate each other along a journey of faith and life."

> "It gives me great joy to listen to them, pray with them and celebrate the Eucharist with them. World Youth Day brings us a message of hope like a pure and youthful breeze," he said.

> Young Catholics can feel alone or ignored, he said, "but they are not alone. Many people of the same age have the same aspirations and, entrusting themselves completely to Christ, they know they have a future before them and are not afraid."

My response to remarks such as "they are not alone," is to ask, with whom do they stand? Who is willing to walk with the young and truly listen to their realities and experiences?

I wouldn't suggest that every experience or preference of

today's young adults needs to be canonized in official ecclesial form, but, at times, the Church collective responds far too slowly to the needs (not just wants, *needs* – spiritual and otherwise), hopes and struggles of young people. This is understandable because the overwhelming majority of Church leaders are significantly older than young adults. And those with the most institutional power tend to be the oldest.

The experiences we have as young men and women definitely shape our historical and spiritual outlooks throughout our lives. One has only to look at the late Pope John Paul II to see how his youthful encounter with the tragic experience of Poland's early 20th-century history shaped his pontifical outlook when it came to matters of justice and the emergence of liberation theology in his senior years. The same can be said about Pope Benedict XVI and his painful experiences as a youth in war-ridden and post-war Germany, as well as the encounters he often cites as a young professor in the late 1960s.

What strikes me about these two examples is that the Church of their youth was not pastorally sensitive to the needs of young people. What I fear as a result is that we are always two or three generations removed from a significant population of the Christian faithful. Instead of truly *listening* to the Church (Body of Christ) of today, which includes youth and young adults, leaders in the Church tend to fall back upon a paternal decreeing of what a young person *should* do or *should not* do, irrespective of their lived realities.

I will say this, Pope Benedict XVI has been extraordinary in his attempts to engage modern technology and social media. He has been outspoken for some time about the Church's need to take seriously these digital advances, always marked, as it were (rightly), with caution.

But there remains much more to be done. And there is a lot more to be heard by way of today's youth and their needs, hopes and struggles. Are we ready to listen?

August 18, 2011

39

The Politics of Insecurity: Forgetting the Holy Spirit

A member of a religious community recently remarked to me: "I believe that the politics in the church have and continue to mirror the politics in America [*sic*], and it doesn't look good." Ostensibly, this person was seeking to convey some reaction to what can be described as an increasingly hostile environment marked as the public sphere is by division and contention. The social, civil and cultural politics are noticeably unsettling — more so in recent years, and this has been observed by news articles and popular commentary. What this person was trying to express is the feeling that ecclesiastical politics, at least as they are popularly experienced, reflect this divisive and contentious sentiment found in the public sphere.

Why is that? What is the cause?

As I've reflected a little on this remark and the truth latently present in such an extemporaneous comment, I have come to realize that at the heart of both shifts in political discourse stands a foundational insecurity. Those who have grown more partisan in terms of the United States social, civil and cultural front have done so as a result of one's fear. Likewise, those who revel in the divisive rhetoric found in analog and virtual public exchanges related to ecclesiastical issues, I believe, do so because of an underlying sense of fear.

The fear is manifold and is likely described in various ways by individuals. Perhaps the shifting sands of a post-enlightenment, postmodern context is too much for some to handle. Perhaps the speed with which communication and travel have become accessible has shrunk the world too much for some who were used to the pace and distance of ages past. Perhaps it's simply a matter of nostalgia, a longing for what once was but is no longer found.

Each camp on each playing field hunkers down in order to establish some foundation amid the seasick motion of life.

The so-called political conservatives talk a talk of values and individual rights as if to suggest the politically progressive lack these traits entirely. Meanwhile the progressive camp launches its own attack against the hypocrisy of its rival, all the while neglecting its own imperfection and incompleteness.

The same is found in the Church. There are some who long for the 1950s as if those were the golden years of American Catholicism, when every priest looked, acted, spoke and sang like Bing Crosby and religious sisters were identifiably dressed in proto-burqas. Yet, as we have since come to realize, the 1950s were plagued by a zephyr of unspoken horror, only recently unveiled in the terrific crimes against innocence and trust. This should not be overlooked. The age is also one of widespread appropriation of stagnant sixteenth-century theology which no longer spoke to the modern world, but was hailed (as it can be today) as the Catholic panacea to the scary reality we call life.

There are those who claim that the Second Vatican Council's legitimate efforts to "update" and "resource" have, on the contrary, not gone far enough. These are those who mark the extreme on yet another side, pointing out the fallacies of those who rally to return to the mythic golden years, only to offer little hopeful response. I find myself often standing on this side of the continuum in ecclesiastical political debates, but I am not yet willing to join the chorus calling for what can be mistaken for a detached ecclesiology or theological reality. The tradition is not to be dismissed, it is to be understood in its appropriate historical context and re-appropriated for today's world.

At the heart of both extremes is the rampant insecurity that internally threatens the emotional, psychological and spiritual safety of the adherents of each respective side. What I believe stands at the root of this insecurity is what I have begun referring to "pneumatological amnesia" (yeah, use *that* phrase at the water cooler – I dare you!). Too many people have simply forgotten about the Holy Spirit.

Those on the so-called conservative side of the camp are so concerned about legislating morality (both civilly and ecclesially) that they act as if they must do everything themselves. Their rhetoric and behavior bespeaks a Pelagian mentality that looks to me like they don't think God can take care of God's self. "If we don't make same-sex unions illegal, God will die!" Is how that sort of insecurity presents itself.

Those on the so-called progressive side of the camp are so concerned about liberty and freedom (both civilly and ecclesially) that they act as if they must do everything themselves. These folks also believe that everything depends on them and that God has stopped working in the world, so they must take matters into their own hands. While this group tends to be well-educated and frequent advocates of historical consciousness, they nevertheless forget that much has changed and developed over some two millennia. Salvation history, Church history, human history are all synonymous. It is God's Spirit that leads and compels, but in God's time, not necessarily yours or mine.

I think we need to all take a deep breath (*ruach* – Spirit) and remember (*memoria* – call-to-mind) that God is not dependent on us. And, meanwhile, God continues to act and move in creation.

What the Letters of St. Paul make so clear time and again is that God's Wisdom *is not OUR wisdom!* God's Will *is not OUR will!* And I think that both the "conservatives" and the "progressives" are going to be surprised to see what God has in store. I know that neither extreme has it correct because, lest we forget, "eye has not see and ear has not heard what God has ready."

When the "opposition" launches a diatribe, ask them and yourself: "Am I living as if I believed in the Holy Spirit?" If your answer is a real "yes," then stop, pray and be open to how God is leading you – it's very likely not in the direction of your original choosing.

July 11, 2011

PART 4

PRAYERS
AND REFLECTIONS ON SCRIPTURE

40

Prayer for the 10th Anniversary of 9/11

God of Our Memories: A Prayer

God of our memories, You have so blessed us with the gift of recollection: To call to mind our joys and hopes, our griefs and anxieties. As we live our lives, it is You who journey with us; As we remember the people, places and events of our lives, it is You who stand by us; And as we commemorate the lives of those who have gone before us, it is Your Spirit that unites us to one another.

At times Your blessing of memory seems like a curse. The remembrances we carry weigh us down like burdens rather than lift our hearts to You. The tragedies, the violence and the sin of our world threaten our ability to see Your presence among us, to experience the breath of life You give us, and to recognize the working of Your Spirit in our lives.

Your Spirit, scripture tells us in the opening of Genesis, moved over the face of the Earth and the chaos of the waters to bring order, life and peace.

Ten years ago we experienced chaos in our lives that stemmed from the reality of sin in our world; Sin marked by violence and hatred and fear. We pray that Your Spirit, which marks the presence of You in our lives, continue to move over the face of the Earth and the chaos of our history. We ask that we might be open to being led by Your Spirit to help renew the face of the Earth, inaugurating order, life and peace.

The memories we carry from ten years ago call to mind the griefs and anxieties, suffering and loss, violence and hatred that reflect that sinful side of our human condition.

Yet, we know that we are more than our limitedness and imperfection. We know that we are called to do more than burnish the mirror of vengeance, or repay hatred with discrimination, or inflict suffering to assuage our own pain. We know that You created us out of love and call us back to our origins. We know that what it means to be created in Your image and likeness is to be peacemakers and lovers in our world.

May we indeed be instruments of Your peace, offering love, pardon, faith, hope, light and joy to the world.

May Your Spirit move over the chaos of our memories and renew the face of our hearts as You continue to renew the face of the Earth. May our memories, the gift you have given us, recall ones once called "enemies" as friends and call to mind those whom we've loved and lost until we share with them the joy of your presence in the life to come.

AMEN.

September 11, 2011

41

An Independence Day Prayer for the 4th of July

Most High, Glorious God,
You are the source of every good thing and You bless Your people with so many gifts.

Those of us who have been born in the nation known as the United States, who by no merit of our own entered this world on this soil, and those who have traveled far and wide to seek the hopes and dreams upon which this nation was founded, are grateful for the opportunities, privileges, protections and lifestyle that this land provides for so many.

On this day during which our collective community of citizens mark the birth of an independent republic, we offer our thanks and praise for those who have dreamed of something beyond tyranny, worked to provide a structure to protect liberty, and fought in defense of the ideal, which proclaims that all women and men were created equal.

Yet, at times we betray our own best interests and those of our forebears. We unwittingly participate in systems that increase inequality, that marginalize minorities, that discriminate against differences, that perpetuates violence at home and abroad.

There is much we can celebrate today, but we do so with a heavy heart aware of our nation's sins and our complicity in that sinfulness.

We proclaim right of liberty for all, but some fight against the rights of others to love, to worship, to live in peace.

We proclaim the right of life for all, but some continue to allow a culture of death for the most vulnerable: the unborn, the elderly and the poorest among us.

We proclaim the right to pursuit happiness for all, but some seek only their own happiness at the expense of others, without regard for the impact of their actions on others, without recognition that there are others.

God of all good things, for these times, we beg forgiveness. We ask that You hear our prayers and help our hearts to be open to Your Spirit, so that we might live more authentically in the manner we proclaim.

We ask that You hear our prayers and help our community, local and national leaders know that their responsibility is the care for *all* the people entrusted to them and that their personal interests should come after the voiceless and vulnerable, and not instead of the concerns of those most in need.

We ask you to hear our prayers and inspire in our whole community of nation the will to be instruments of peace, reconcilers of the human family, and leaders in forgiving the trespasses committed against us. Only then, Lord, we know that we can be forgiven for all that we have and continue to do to harm others, at home and abroad.

This is indeed the day that you have made and it is right and just that we rejoice and celebrate it. May we not come to mistake nation for you, patriotism for faith, and liberty for the true freedom that only comes from you.

Bless us, we pray, and bless the whole world, that what is good about our national community might be shared with others, what is good about other nations might be a model for us, and that the whole world might someday rejoice at its collective independence from the tyranny of human power and greed, and celebrate its joyful dependence on You.

We ask all these things, on this Independence Day, in Your Name.

AMEN.

July 4, 2012

42

A Peace Prayer for Norway and the World

As so many suffer in Oslo, Norway this day, victims of violence in our world, the Church, which is the Body of Christ, can come together to pray for our sisters and brothers in the human family.

No amount of consoling words, retributive promises or military action will make up for the senseless loss of life, but we know that our prayers do not go unheard and that grieving hearts seek peace. In this moment of suffering and pain, perhaps we can find some hopeful assurance in a world where hatred is replaced with love, injury is replaced with forgiveness and despair is overcome by hope.

For all those who seek words to express the emotional maelstrom of fear and loss, I offer you an alternative setting to the famous peace prayer that has been for so long associated with Francis of Assisi. Even though he was not in fact its author, it expresses much that he demonstrated with his life and the approach to Gospel life that bears his name.

Lord Jesus Christ, make us people of your peace; in the furrows plowed by hate, let us sow love; Let us bathe the injured with Mercy; be sign of faith to the doubting; open the door for the desperate; strike a light in the darkness; and teach the sad to laugh again.

Lord Jesus Christ, grant that we may not so much grasp at being consoled as to console; at being understood as to understand; at being loved as to love; for it is in giving that we receive, it is in forgiving that we are forgiven, and it is in dying that we are free to live.

AMEN.

July 22, 2011

43

The Meaning of Prayer

In today's Gospel (Matthew 6:7-15) Jesus tells his disciples and us today *how* to pray. But *what* does the prayer mean? This is at first a little hard to pin-point for those who have repeated the prayer known to us as the Our Father, which Jesus passes on to us and which is remembered in today's Gospel. Familiarity sometimes results in a glossing over of the details of what we know so well, blinding us — innocently as it were — to the powerful meaning behind the words that have been handed down to us.

In the case of the Our Father, the *way* of prayer with

which Jesus instructs us today, there are three parts to the prayer that help us to understand what it is we are actually doing. The first part of the prayer is the address, the naming of God as the receiver of our prayer, our communication, and our petition. "Our Father, Who art in Heaven, Hallowed (holy) is your name." We make it clear, at Jesus's command, who it is we are addressing.

The second part is nearly as brief, this is the petition, the request, the "meat" of our prayer. "Thy Kingdom come, Thy Will be done." To some this might be one of the more overlooked dimensions of the prayer, but this is an important, if brief, hinge or linchpin to the prayer. I remember one of my scripture professors in graduate school telling us that these two lines are the whole point of Christian living and the centerpiece of the prayer. Our petition is that we, in praying the prayer and following Christ, are asking for the in-breaking of the Kingdom of God. This is not a passive request, something we simply ask God to do *for us*. Instead, the second phrase "Thy Will Be Done," is the explanation of how God's Kingdom comes.

As Christians, as those baptized into a unique relationship with Christ and one another, we are the instruments of God's peace and reign in the world. God's Kingdom becomes manifest in the little ways, the actions and decisions we make daily that reflect God's Will. Doing God's Will is how the Kingdom Comes. So, you're probably wondering, what is God's Will? What does it look like? That's the remaining part of the prayer!

Part Three is the descriptive section that illustrates what God's Kingdom looks like, how the world and our relationships appear when we are doing God's Will. Earth begins to look like Heaven, everybody's bodily and spiritual needs are fulfilled (daily bread), our sins are forgiven just as we have forgiven all those who sin against us, we are no longer led into temptation (greed, selfishness, and all the associated dispositions that tempt us to break relationship), and we are ultimately delivered from evil.

St. Francis of Assisi knew this intuitively, even though he didn't earn a master's or doctorate in scripture. He didn't know Greek and wasn't a Christian historian. Yet, he knew and modeled for us a way of life that recognized that prayer was so much more than a bunch of words (the babbling that Jesus rejects early in today's Gospel). Prayer was communication with God and communication happens in more ways than just speaking, but also in our actions — it's true: actions *do speak louder* than words!

Francis wrote a commentary (an *expositio*) on the Our Father, a reflection inspired by the prayer that Jesus left us. In his reflection, Francis concludes the brief section on "Your will be done on earth as in heaven" with the following extended prayer:

> And may we love our neighbor as ourselves by drawing them all to Your love with our whole strength, by rejoicing in the good of others as in our own, by suffering with others at their misfortunes, and by giving offense to no one. (*Expositio in Pater Noster,* v. 5)

May our prayer today, and always, be after the instruction of Jesus in today's Gospel — aware that our prayer is best prayed by the actions of our lives in the way that Francis highlights in his reflection. That in doing God's Will and striving to recall that in our everyday lives, we might truly help usher in the Kingdom of God.

June 21, 2012

44

Do You Recognize the Risen Lord?

Easter brings with it an abundance of natural joy and reason for celebration. The love of God poured out for us through the Incarnation, the life, the death and now the resurrection, which today we commemorate, of Jesus of Nazareth is made known in the most powerful ways. The resurrection is a focal point of our faith, without which the crucifixion would have no more meaning than the another innocent man executed by the state. The Incarnation, the entering of God into the world as one like us, which we commemorate at Christmas, is another focal point — a calling to mind God's humility and care for us. So much does God love us that God entered our world as one like us. Now that is love!

One of the things that the Scripture has called my attention to this Easter is the number of ways the friends and disciples of Jesus do and do not recognize the risen Lord. Have you ever noticed that? Why is it that? What were they expecting to see? What are *we* expecting to see?

The message from God — sent by, literally, "messengers from God" (*angels*) — is "Do not be afraid" (Matt 28:5), "Do not be amazed" (Mark 16: 6), "Why do you seek the living among the dead?" (Luke 24:5) and "Why are you weeping?" (John 20:13). There is, at first glance, a lot of confusion and the need for a messenger from God to begin to clarify the situation, reset the context, for it had only been a few days since the Lord was crucified. He was supposed to be dead, or so they thought.

What do we think? What do we expect? What do God's messengers, God's mediators need to say to us?

I stood at before the crowd yesterday in New York City and, during one of my seven reflections on the last words of Christ, mentioned that the Good News according to Luke is my favorite of the Gospels. One of the myriad reasons for this is the way the text ends. The account of the walk to Emmaus is by far one of the most powerful stories in all of the New Testament.

It is a story of the confusion of human expectations, we clearly do not know what is going on sometimes. What at first seems like a tragedy, like an end — a crucifixion perhaps — suddenly becomes a sign from God and a confirmation of Kingdom that the Risen Lord preached in his words and demonstrated with his deeds. Yet, how do we come to recognize the Risen Lord?

This Easter, this is my reflection: How do I recognize the Risen Lord? In the breaking of the bread? In the sharing of the Good News? In the entering into relationship with another? How is it that the disciples and friends of the Lord came to recognize him?

Here is the full text of the Emmaus story. Have a Blessed Easter and may you come to recognize the Risen Lord in your life!

The Road to Emmaus

That very day, the first day of the week, two of Jesus' disciples were going to a village seven miles from Jerusalem called Emmaus, and they were conversing about all the things that had occurred. And it happened that while they were conversing and debating, Jesus himself drew near and walked with them, but their eyes were prevented from recognizing him.

He asked them, "What are you discussing as you walk along?" They stopped, looking downcast.

One of them, named Cleopas, said to him in reply, "Are you the only visitor to Jerusalem who does not know of the things that have taken place there in these days?"

And he replied to them, "What sort of things?"

They said to him, "The things that happened to Jesus the Nazarene, who was a prophet mighty in deed and word before God and all the people, how our chief priests and rulers both handed him over to a sentence of death and crucified him. But we were hoping that he would be the one to redeem Israel; and besides all this, it is now the third day since this took place. Some women from our group, however, have astounded us: they were at the tomb early in the morning and did not find his body; they came back and reported that they had indeed seen a vision of angels who announced that he was alive. Then some of those with us went to the tomb and found things just as the women had described, but him they did not see."

And he said to them, "Oh, how foolish you are! How slow of heart to believe all that the prophets spoke! Was it not necessary that the Christ should suffer these things and enter into his glory?"

Then beginning with Moses and all the prophets, he interpreted to them what referred to him in all the Scriptures.

As they approached the village to which they were going, he gave the impression that he was going on farther. But they urged him, "Stay with us, for it is nearly evening and the day is almost over."

So he went in to stay with them. And it happened that, while he was with them at table, he took bread, said the blessing, broke it, and gave it to them.

With that their eyes were opened and they recognized him, but he vanished from their sight. Then they said to each other,

"Were not our hearts burning within us while he spoke to us on the way and opened the Scriptures to us?" So they set out at once and returned to Jerusalem where they found gathered together the eleven and those with them who were saying,

"The Lord has truly been raised and has appeared to Simon!" Then the two recounted what had taken place on the way and how he was made known to them in the breaking of bread. (Luke 24:13-35)

April 23, 2011

45

Restless Hearts and Being Made for God

I've been thinking a lot about some of the most famous theological thinkers in Christian history and their description of what it means to be a human person. Among the several characteristics that these thinkers identify is the intrinsic or inherent capacity for God that all human beings have. What's more interesting than noting the *possibility* that we have to be in relationship with God (what Karl Rahner would describe as humanity as *capax Dei*), is that most of these classic theologians assert that we are — as with the rest of creation — *intended* for the Divine. This is perhaps most classically expressed by St. Augustine of Hippo, in his *Confessions*, where he wrote:

> You awaken us to delight in Your praise; for You made us for Yourself, and our heart is restless, until it rests in Thee (*Confessions*, Book I).

Here we come to see that, for Augustine, human beings have been created precisely for relationship with God. It is only God that can satisfy the longing our hearts express. We strive so often to fulfill our deepest desires with all sorts of other things: money, power, control, success, and so on. Yet, the wisdom that Augustine reveals is that these things — no matter how much we attain — cannot meet our most fundamental longing.

One way we might consider our finite human quest to satisfy our restless hearts with things other than God is to talk about having a "disordered" appetite. The term "disordered" sounds extraordinarily judgmental and, when wielded carelessly, can often be used to hurt people and express moral disdain. However, "disordered" attempts to satisfy our longing for God is simply another way to talk about manifold selfishness, or making our self the ultimate goal or end of our energies.

The notion of this "disordered" attempt to quench our longing for the Divine is presented in the work of Blessed John Duns Scotus, one of my favorite medieval thinkers and a fellow Franciscan friar. In his *De Primo Principio*, a rather philosophical (albeit frequently prayerful) treatise on God as "First Principle," Scotus draws the conclusion that "Nothing whatever is essentially ordered to itself" (*De Primo Principio* 2.2).

What the Subtle Doctor helps us to recall here is that we are not created to serve only ourselves. Fundamentally, we have lovingly been brought into existence to experience and enter into relationship with God, one another, and all of creation. Scotus goes on to explain that, in the case of the Divine, God is both our cause and our end, our Creator and our Goal.

What does this have to do with us? What is the wisdom Augustine and Scotus offer us today?

I think it can be very tempting and, at times, difficult to avoid thinking about ourselves first. Our culture is very individualistic and purports that our primary duty is to self, but our Christian tradition claims something rather different. We believe just the opposite. Yes, we have a responsibility to care for ourselves (Thomas Aquinas talks about this in terms of the natural inclination to survive), but we also have a responsibility for others.

This responsibility to care for others stems from our ultimate goal, which is understood as communion or an increasingly intimate relationship with God. Remembering that God is our true end, our ultimate goal, that for which we have been created, de-centers our ego from the reality of our own construction and places us squarely back within the "ordered" (to borrow Scotus's philosophical term) world.

In what ways do we need to reconsider our priorities and worldview? Is our default mode to put ourselves first and then, if we have extra time, money, or energy, care for others? Or do we live in a manner reflecting the rightly ordered interdependence into which God has placed us? Do we allow our hearts to rest in God or do we seek another place to dwell?

August 13, 2012

46

Heaven is Not a Vacation

During the retreat this weekend, while looking at the model of St. Francis of Assisi for Christian living today, a question was asked by a retreatant about how we can come to know what is needed to get to heaven. In response, I found myself making the distinction between a pilgrimage and a vacation. A vacation usually includes a destination where someone would like to go and plans to visit. The focus is on the place and the vacationer is most concerned with arriving and spending as much time as possible at the destination, avoiding delays are travel snafus while traveling to ensure that the maximum amount of time and enjoyment at the destination takes place. It seems that a lot of people like to think of heaven much like they think of a vacation. They just want to get there. They want to get there quickly, without trouble and know with certainty that their path there is the most direct. Yet, I'm much more convinced that what we call heaven is better thought of as like a pilgrimage.

A lot of folks have been talking about Martin Sheen's new movie *The Way,* which I intend to see but haven't had the chance yet (as an aside, Martin Sheen is a professed Secular Franciscan and a committed Roman Catholic who has been engaged in lots of social-justice work — not your typical Hollywood type, nor your typical crazy Hollywood "catholic" á la Mel Gibson). One of the tag lines for the *The Way* is "Life is about the Journey." This is precisely the point of heaven.

The movie *The Way* features a father setting out on a pilgrimage, following in the footsteps of his deceased son. It is perhaps one of the most famous and frequently traveled pilgrimages in the world: "Camino de Santiago, also known as The Way of Saint James," in Spain. What the movie tag line reminds us, at least in part, is that a pilgrimage is very different from a vacation. Both have destinations, but whereas a vacation is about the destination, a pilgrimage is just as much (if not more) about the journey.

On pilgrimage you always keep the destination, the goal, the endpoint in mind, but your journey there becomes the privileged place of prayer and reflection. On the way to a vacation, the journey or travel can be a burden and a cumbersome necessity, but on a pilgrimage the journey or travel is the whole point.

Life is a pilgrimage, not a vacation. Heaven might very well be the destination, the goal, the endpoint, but that *telos* should inform and shade our journey there. It should help us to see the path along which we travel in a new light, not one of utility or "counting down the minutes" until we arrive at our destination, but instead add meaning and life along our way.

Keeping in mind who we are, who we were created to be and with whom we were created to be in relationship, our journey is a pilgrimage of love and life, not a cosmic plane ride on which we should simply pass the time by sleeping, zoning out, watching a crappy movie or reading a mediocre novel. We should walk the way, connecting along the path with others on the journey of life, because we are all on the same pilgrimage toward God.

Thinking of heaven like a vacation allows us to disconnect from ourselves, others and God, while thinking of heaven as a pilgrimage reminds us of the gift of journey and the Divine encounters we can experience along the way.

October 17, 2011

47

Recognizing the Samuel and Eli in Each of Us

Success!
More money!
A New House!
A promotion!
Happiness!

Love!

Jesus question to the two disciples of John in today's Gospel is a question he still poses to us today: *What are you looking for?*

Most of us don't have a very clear answer to that question. So often we're not very sure what we're looking for and in our uncertainty we might latch onto things, ideas or goals that miss the point. We might *think* we know what it is, but are we mistaken?

In this way we can relate to the young Samuel in the first reading. He hears God calling him, but doesn't quite get it. He *thinks* he knows what he's looking for, that Eli has called him in the night. Running to Eli, Samuel *thinks* he's got it – but Eli tells him that he's confused and needs to go back to bed. This happens again and Samuel still doesn't get it.

It finally dawns on Eli what is happening, that it is God who is calling Samuel to something. That God was present the whole time, but Samuel could not recognize the call of the one who is always with him. Samuel did not know, until Eli finally recognized what was happening, *what it was he was looking for.*

Aren't we like that a lot? Aren't we like Samuel? We say every Sunday in the Creed that: "I believe in God…I believe in Jesus Christ…I believe in the Holy Spirit," but how often do we fail to recognize God calling us in our own lives?

This is one of the problems I think we face in our own time. It's certainly a problem that I face. There is so much to distract us from God and from our spiritual lives, from what is so obvious and near to us, and from what is really, truly important.

I am, like so many of you, a person deeply steeped in technology. Most of us have to be *on*line, *on* our blackberries or iPhones, *on* the conference calls, *on* Facebook, *on* Twitter, on, on, on!

I am "on" as much as the next guy… and, while these things are good, these things are part of life, and this work is important; these things also distract me many times from hearing the voice of God in my own life.

So often I can feel like Samuel, recognizing something calling me, nudging me, trying to get my attention…but then in my distraction and busy-ness I confuse what is probably the

Spirit of God in my life for something else. And I just go back to sleep.

How about you? Do you find a stirring within your heart and mind, feel a sense of God's call in your life, but don't recognize it because you are *too busy* or *too distracted* or *just unsure of what you are looking for?*

And then there's the case of Eli.

Oh yes, Eli. Most people hear this first reading proclaimed and think immediately of Samuel, because we are all in some ways a little bit like Samuel. But, aren't we also like Eli?

See, Eli is the wisdom figure here.

Eli is the "go-to-guy" for Samuel, the problem solver in this case. But he misses the mark too. It takes Samuel waking Eli up *three times* — which is, let's face it, a lot of interrupted sleep – before he recognizes that God is working in this young man's life.

It is our responsibility, our duty as members of the Christian community to do what Eli should have done from the beginning – to help others to see how God is calling them in their particular lives.

We believe that God is working in *everybody's* lives, whether they see it or not, whether they recognize the voice of God or not.

Everybody is being *called by God* as Samuel was, called to live the Gospel in different ways...ways that reflect the gifts and talents, the challenges and struggles, the opportunities and pitfalls we face in our lives.

We are, in a sense, too often like Samuel unable to easily recognize God's calling in our lives, but we are also like Eli who fail so often to see how God is working in others' lives.

Which brings us back to the Gospel and Jesus's question to the two disciples of John the Baptist who have begun to follow this Jesus guy. *What are you looking for?*

I think it's very interesting that after Jesus recognizes that these two strange men are now hanging around him, he doesn't ask: "who are you?" But instead, "what are you looking for?"

And, neither of them answers his question. Neither Andrew nor the unnamed disciple is able to say *what exactly* he is looking for in following Jesus.

And this should not be surprising, because they simply do not know. The only way they can know is to respond to the invitation that Jesus then extends: *Come, and you will see!*

It's true that we don't *really* know what we're looking for either. And the only way we're going to find out is to do what the disciples did and "*come and see.*"

After the disciples take up Jesus's invitation to "come and see," they get it – they *find what they were looking for* – and announce it to other: "We have found the Messiah!"

We have found the savior, we have found the one we didn't even know we were looking for, but he has called us into a new way of living. And their lives have changed from that point on. Have ours? Do we live differently? Do we proclaim by *our actions* and *our words* and *our outlook on life* that we too have found the messiah?

This means giving up the false things that distract us from what we should *really* be looking for; This means being more attentive to how God is calling us in our own lives; This means helping others to recognize the ways in which God is calling them in their lives.

What this all amounts to is understanding our *vocation* – how it is God is calling us to live.

While most people think of vocation in terms of religious and priests like those of us in these medieval hooded brown outfits, vocation is much larger and everyone has one. This is what it means to be called by God, like Samuel in the Night, like us in our time.

Thomas Merton, the Trappist Monk and famous Spiritual writer 1950s and 1960s, explains that the term vocation is much more rich than we usually give it credit. He wrote:

> Each one of us has some kind of vocation. We are called by God to share in God's Life and Kingdom. Each one of us is called to a special place in the Kingdom. If we find that place we will be happy. If we do not find it, we can never be completely happy. For each one of us, there is only one thing necessary: to fulfill our own destiny according to God's will, to be what *God wants us to be.*

To "Be what God wants us to be," to "find our vocation," is to truly find *what it is we are looking for.* And we do that by taking seriously Jesus's invitation to each of us, here and now, to *Come, and follow him, and SEE.*

January 15, 2012

48

The Spirit of Truth:
Sometimes God Tells us What we Don't Want to Hear

Today's Gospel (John 14:15-21) is often read as a sign of hope and promise. It tells of Jesus's promise to send the Spirit to be with and guide the Body of Christ, which is the Church. He promises that his followers will not be left orphans, but that he will remain with us and come to us. In way so typical of John, this discourse of Jesus is almost a riddle. He concludes with this series of thoughts:

> "On that day you will realize that I am in my Father and you are in me and I in you. Whoever has my commandments and observes them is the one who loves me. And whoever loves me will be loved by my Father, and I will love him and reveal myself to him."

> Yet, it is his explanation of the sending of the Spirit that I think gets too quickly glossed over and something that we should really pause and consider today.

> And I will ask the Father, and he will give you another Advocate to be with you always, the Spirit of truth, whom the world cannot accept, because it neither sees nor knows him. But you know him, because he remains with you, and will be in you.

The work of the Spirit of God is unrecognizable to the world — is it no wonder that we so often forget God's presence in our history and creation? The more we become "of the world," the less likely we are to recognize God in our everyday lives.

Sometimes, I think, we expect the presence of God in our lives to appear like a miraculous event, something out of the ordinary, but as Jesus tells us in the Gospel, the Spirit is always already with us and — let's not forget — *in us* ("and will be *in you*"). How do we listen to God's Spirit in us? Do we listen to God's Spirit in us?

What Jesus says about the Spirit with and in us is a lot like what we know of the Kingdom of God and the Wisdom of God (and "wisdom" is a Scriptural term going back to the Old Testament that is a symbol of Divine immanence). What we hear in John's Gospel is an echo of what we hear from St. Paul that the Good News, the proclamation of the Kingdom, is foolishness, stupidity, a stumbling block to those of this world. What does this mean?

Frankly, I believe it means that oftentimes God tells us what we don't want to hear. The Spirit of God works build up the Body of Christ, the Church, not tear it down. When we speak or act in ways that breaks relationship, we are not recognizing the Spirit. When we support and participate in systems of violence, war or injustice, we are not recognizing the Spirit. When we choose to ignore the outcast, the marginalized, the poor, the different, we are not recognizing the Spirit.

Recognizing the Spirit with and in us requires an openness on our part to surrendering the self-centeredness that the world promotes and a willingness to follow Christ, *truly* follow Christ as we bear His Name. It may seems like foolishness — nonviolence, love, justice, forgiveness — but it is what God is telling us to do. That is, after all, why the Holy Spirit is called by Jesus "the Spirit of Truth."

May 29, 2011

49

Making the Ordinary Extraordinary in Ordinary Time

Well it's that time of year again, the first week of "Ordinary Time" in the Liturgical Year. Like so much about the English language, the way we translate this season of the Church year — "ordinary" — leaves much to be desired and, due to the oftentimes limited nuance in our native tongue, does not necessarily convey what is originally intended. Instead of "plain" or "unimportant," as the word ordinary is generally used in the common dialogue, one should think of the Latin source of the term *Ordo*, meaning order, ranking, structure, system. Ordinary Time does not mean that the season is insignificant or "downtime" from the more "important" periods in the liturgical cycle of the Church year. Rather, it is a structured or *ordered* time, demarcated weekly by a sequential numbering, in which we live out our Christian life and listen to Sacred Scripture expound on the mysteries we celebrate as members of the Body of Christ.

In what might strike some as plain or ordinary, the cyclic valleys in between the liturgical mountains of Advent, Christmas, Lent and Easter on the dynamic landscape of the Church Year, should offer us an opportunity to reflect more deeply on the structure and order of time. Time is a sacred dimension that marks our journeys of faith and life. Time, as Albert Einstein keenly posited, is not simply a constant of absolute measurement as it once was conceived, but a dynamic and relative dimension of reality that is integrally connected to space. What that might mean for Christians is that we cannot simply dismiss the fourth dimension of reality, Time, as irrelevant as we selectively focus on the (at least) three physical dimensions of our existence, but instead recognize that Time is also an aspect of creation that God intentionally designed.

Like all of creation, Time is holy and our marking the passage of Time should play a role in our prayer and spiritual lives. In a sense, all Time then is extraordinary, so let's live that way. Even the minutes you "waste" daydreaming or zoning out are precious gifts of life, there's really nothing *ordinary* about them.

January 10, 2012

50

Providing Good Ground for the Word

There is a risk that today's First Reading might take a back seat to the Gospel, which is Matthew's account of the Our Father, so I think it's important for us to take just a moment to consider what is being presented to us in Scripture from the Prophet Isaiah. The imagery might not seem all that relevant or even appealing to those unfamiliar with farming or gardening (as I am most certainly not, I have never been good at keeping plants alive), but there is great wisdom that can speak to our experiences today and guide us on our Lenten journey.

> Thus says the LORD: Just as from the heavens the rain and snow come down And do not return there till they have watered the earth, making it fertile and fruitful, Giving seed to the one who sows and bread to the one who eats, So shall my word be that goes forth from my mouth; It shall not return to me void, but shall do my will, achieving the end for which I sent it. (Is 55:10-11)

The operative image of agricultural flourishing might not immediately strike the modern listener given our technological way of living in the world and the degree to which so many of us are removed from the production of our food. Yet, there are simple aspects that the original hearers may have taken for granted that help us to appreciate more deeply what is being revealed here.

For one thing, a productive crop requires several factors to be present and effective. There must be sunlight, rain, the planting of seed, the right balance of ground and air temperature and the like. All of these things come together to produce the right environment from which crops will grow. It is at that point one can judge the ground as fertile and good.

Isaiah communicates the perspective of the Lord in such language in order to get us to think about the myriad factors that coalesce to provide the "good ground" necessary for the Word of God to produce fruit in our lives. What might not be easily seen at first in this passage is that we are told God always already provides those things necessary for the tilling of good ground, just as God always already provides the rain and sun. But we are not like ordinary ground in which the seed of a vegetable or fruit is planted. We are a living ground that effects its own ability to be good or bad for the seed planted within our hearts.

God's Word is revealed to us and, while God's grace — like the sun and rain — is already offered to us, we have the freedom to accept or reject it. We have the freedom to be good ground for the Word or not.

During this season of Lent, when we take time to pause and reflect on the factors of the spiritual life that come together and are offered to us by God, perhaps we can consider the ways in which we do or do not allow that Grace to take hold of our lives and provide good ground for the Word.

February 28, 2012

51

On Writing as Co-Creating with God

I am not an artist.

I have had the great privilege to know many artists and I know that I am simply not to be counted among them. I have the greatest respect for someone who can take the matters of creation and shape, color or mold them into expressions of something far greater than the sum of their various parts – paper, wood, pigment, oil, etc. It would not surprise me if an artist understood her work as an expression or exercise of her vocation as one created *Imago Dei*, a co-creator in the world. But I am not an artist, I don't know about that.

I am a writer. Over the years I've found myself more and more engaged in the process of writing. It began with some popular and then more-scholarly essays. I then was drawn deeper into areas of Franciscan, Mertonian, and Systematic research. I wrote to understand and I wrote to share what I learned. I continue to write for both those reasons, but also realize that much of my drive – the Spirit? (as in: the One who *drives* Jesus into the desert in Mark's Gospel) – compels and informs my understanding and engagement with words.

There is a fine line between drive and compulsion, a line that is very often difficult to see.

Recently, I've started to appreciate how much I *love* to write (perhaps like an iconographer loves to paint). It might sound silly, and I certainly feel a bit vulnerable sharing this perhaps perceptible reality, but it's a relatively new realization for me. It's come to the fore of my thoughts in large part because of how I've found myself engaged in several writing projects in recent months that have been both challenging and life-giving.

There are the three books, each in various stages of completion, one set to come out in the Spring and another the following Fall. There is the longer-term edition of the correspondence of Thomas Merton and Naomi Burton Stone, which is a book project all together different from what I'm used to. There is a newer effort also in the works. There are the dozens of essays, some popular, some invited chapters in books, still others slated for journals or magazines. There are the conference papers and the invited lectures that require a different style of writing, one that allows me to also anticipate my voice.

Finally, there is the blog. The latest iteration of my writing and one about which I remain somewhat ambivalent. While not my original idea, I have come to both love and regret this medium. There is much to love including the many with whom I've been connected since its launch and the opportunity to write daily, express myself through so many thousands and thousands of words.

Writing, I've come to appreciate, is one of the truest

forms of the human vocation to be a co-creator with God.

To write is, in a sense, to create *ex nihilo* in a way other artistic or human endeavors do not. A painter or sculptor manipulates matter into an aesthetic creation reflecting the beauty of God, the soul of the artist and the imagination of the viewer.

But the writer takes thoughts and images, previously unexpressed, and ex-presses them – pushes them outward – into the world. As I can see a blank sheet of paper or a blinking word-processing cursor, there is nothing there, nothing external to mold in quite the same way as in the other media. As the thoughts come, the keys are stroked or the pen glides by, signifiers are set down that take on a life of their own.

A manuscript draft can be reshaped and remolded, but the creation of those previously non-existent raw materials seems to me to be a co-creation with God. The gift of human language is indeed, like all human gifts, finite and capable of subjection to hubris and abuse. But the potential for something greater is in itself an astounding beauty to me.

So, to those who feel the drive of the Spirit to express yourself in written word, know that you are in solidarity with the others similarly moved by God. To those who have been so generous with your time, support, feedback, comments, invitations to dialogue or speak, offer of critique and demonstration of patience with my writing – thank you.

To those who find writing to be laborious or boring, know that your use is elsewhere and your medium is one of the myriad dimensions of human creativity – be open to the Spirit's work in your life. For those who, for that reason or others, suspect that my writing fits that bill, an enterprise of endurance rather than a labor of love, rest assured that fewer things seem to give me as much joy in these recent years. I pray that is might continue for years to come.

June 20, 2011

52

Jesus, Peter, and the Meaning of "Love"

One of my favorite musicians, Jason Mraz, has recently released a new studio album with the title "Love is a Four Letter Word." It's a clever title, as Mraz usually provides, which highlights the power of love as a word with the force of the more infamous "four-letter words," we are more accustomed to recognize. This phrase is right to the point and insightful, if only "love" was indeed a four-letter word. In English it is. However, in the Greek of John's Gospel, from which we get today's reading, there are several words that are used for what in English we call love. There is *agape, eros*, and *philia*, just to name three. In the Gospel passage Peter is confused, it would seem, by what Jesus is asking — so too, we are easily confused by what Jesus asks Peter and Peter's response to the Lord in John 21: 15-19: "Do you *love* me?"

While the English translation can only present the word "love" in each instance, there are in fact several different words being used – *agape* and *philia* are the two in play, to be exact.

Jesus asks Peter: "Do you *agape*?" Referring to the selfless, sacrificial love that is modeled by Jesus of Nazareth himself in loving the unlovable, forgiving the unforgivable, embracing the neglected, forgotten and voiceless. *Agape* is a love beyond all telling, offering a peace the world cannot give.

Yet, to Jesus's question, Peter responds, "Of Course, Lord, I *philia!*" This is a type of love that is more associated with friendship or family, it is the affection that one has for another that one cares about or loves in the most typical way.

Jesus asks if Peter is willing, able, practicing the love that the Son of God has called his followers to exercise, and Peter is responding with an admittance of a different kind of love, the love of affection.

Jesus asks Peter a second time if he loves in the sense of *agape*, and Peter responds as before: *philia*. The third time Jesus changes the type of love, supposedly now recognizing where Peter stands and how he is capable of loving at the time. He, in one sense, confirms the love that Peter has.

But the encounter doesn't stop there. Jesus offers this brief parable about being a young man and becoming an old man. He tells Peter that the love he can give at this point (*philia*) is a reflection of what he wants, what he is capable of at the time, and it is — in a non-derogatory sense — an *immature* love. It is a love in need of growth and conversion.

It's easy to love in the sense of *philia*, but it is very, very difficult to love in the sense of *agape*. Jesus's *agape* led to giving his whole self, even until death, death on a cross. The closing line of this Gospel passage is "Follow Me," challenging Peter – *and us!* — to surrender ourselves to the love we are called to embrace and practice. We can easily love those we like and care about, standing with Peter in our current state of Christian living. But it is not the end and *philia* is not enough to follow in the footprints of Christ.

May we embrace the invitation and challenge of Jesus to follow him, growing in love from *philia* to *agape*. Only then will we realize that Love is so much more than a four-letter word.

May 25, 2012

53

What God Desires from Us

This morning's reading from the Book of the Prophet Micah is perhaps one of the most important passages from among all of the Hebrew Scriptures. In it we hear the prophet present God's plea to the people, exasperated at the ostensible hard-headedness of humanity. We just don't seem to get it. In every generation, for thousands of years, women and men seem to struggle to discover and understand what it is that God wants from them or how it is God wants them to live. Yet, God says through Micah, you already know the answer, it's right before you. Here is the full text of today's First Reading (Micah 6:1-4, 6-8) it's not that long:

Hear what the LORD says: Arise, present your plea before the mountains, and let the hills hear your voice! Hear, O mountains, the plea of the LORD, pay attention, O foundations of the earth! For the LORD has a plea against his people, and he enters into trial with Israel.

O my people, what have I done to you, or how have I wearied you? Answer me! For I brought you up from the land of Egypt, from the place of slavery I released you; and I sent before you Moses, Aaron, and Miriam.

With what shall I come before the LORD, and bow before God most high? Shall I come before him with burnt offerings, with calves a year old? Will the LORD be pleased with thousands of rams, with myriad streams of oil? Shall I give my first-born for my crime, the fruit of my body for the sin of my soul? You have been told, O man, what is good, and what the LORD requires of you: Only to do the right and to love goodness, and to walk humbly with your God.

It's important to notice at the beginning of the reading that God calls upon the rest of creation to serve as the witness in a formal, almost courtroom-like scene. There is a value and dignity placed upon the otherwise ordinary aspects of the landscape and earth that is overlooked by most people. But not God. God sees in creation a relational quality that functions here like a sibling to or peer of humanity, like a jury of our peers.

The complaint or frustration on God's part is that we have been given so much, everything has been made so clear, and we have had all the guidance and instruction we could desire, yet we still don't "get it."

Micah recounts the great prophets and includes both men *and* women (Miriam is added to Moses and Aaron). And the rest of the prophetic and patristic tradition is implied, but we still are lost. We try to do what *we think we should*, which far too often is our own projection or reflects our own interest.

Is it more sacrifice that God desires? Does God want our best work, the fruit of our labors? Is God interested in what we can give from our abundance or even our poverty? Would God prefer us, like Abraham, to offer our first born, our children? Does God want me to go to daily mass, pray more rosaries, participate in more novenas, or go to exposition of the Blessed Sacrament more often?

No. God wants none of these things, Scripture tells us. Whether it's in the form of ancient sacrifice or in some contemporary iteration of the same thing, God is clear that these all miss the mark in some way. It's not that offering one's gifts or talents, participating in daily mass or praying a certain way is inherently bad, it isn't. However, those might better *serve us.*

But what does *God Want?*

And Micah tells us. It's so simple, yet implies so much and demands even more from us.

Only to do the right and to love goodness, and to walk humbly with your God.

July 23, 2012

54

The "Spiritual Low-Carb Diet" and the Bread of Life

What is that you do when all you really want is the "bread of life" and the world around you only offers a "spiritual low-carb diet?"

It will come as no surprise, especially to those who live or vacation along the Jersey Shore where I'm ministering in a parish this summer, that our popular culture is obsessed with body image and weight gain. In recent years the so-called "low-carb diets" have become very popular, whether in the form of the "Atkins Diet" or some other plan, people have become very hostile toward foods rich in carbohydrates, especially *bread!*

This is significant because for the next several weeks we'll be hearing a lot about bread in the Sunday Gospel accounts. It begins this weekend.

Whereas the miracles in this Sunday's First Reading and Gospel would appear as a glorious gift from God for those hungering for the energy-rich bread they've been given, I bet that there are plenty of people in our modern North American, United States context that find the idea of abundant loaves — with leftovers to fill a dozen baskets — much-less appealing.

"Um...oh...lots of bread. Thank you, Jesus, but I'm going to have to pass, I'm on a low-carb diet! Do you have any meat?"

On the one hand this miracle seems like a very obvious one to interpret: lots of people are around, they get hungry, the generosity of God through the sharing of others makes it possible for all to eat their fill.

Yet, on the other hand, I think this miracle story provides us with a modern allegory. It's a metaphor for what I want to call the "spiritual low-carb diet" that is all the rage these days in our popular culture.

One point of the story is the over abundance of food available, the amazing quantity of bread right at one's fingertips. Similarly, God's grace and love is over abundant and surrounds us, it is everywhere and also at our fingertips. However, in a culture that finds carbs distasteful, bread is shunned or ignored. Likewise, in a culture that finds faith distasteful, the grace and love of God that surrounds us is shunned or ignored.

Have we become self-conscious about our faith and our desire to have the bread of life, which is Jesus Christ? Is there a sense in which the popular culture discourages us from that want, making us think that we can "do it ourselves" without God or substitute faith with some other low-carb version of belief?

Just like the distaste for bread and other carb-rich foods, the distaste for God and the practice of faith is a luxury of the affluent who convince themselves that they no longer need God. Such a context reminds me of Mother Teresa's saying about a different type of poverty among the comfortable in the world, she said: "The hunger for love is much more difficult to remove than the hunger for bread."

We all hunger for love, the love of one another and the love of God.

What then is the miracle in today's readings about in our particular context? Is it about bread? Or might it be about the abundant love of God everywhere, overflowing, present at our fingertips?

Jesus doesn't make bread out of thin air. He takes what little is offered by a stranger, food brought forward to share with those who have none, and turns it into a tremendous feast.

The same is true with God in our world. The Lord can take what little love, what little kindness, what little generosity we can offer and turn it into a feast full of the bread of life at the table of plenty.

Following Mother Teresa, we should certainly work to remove the hunger of bellies in our world, but what are we doing about the spiritual hunger for love in our midst? Which of us is going to step forward and make a difference?

July 29, 2012

55

Seeing with the Eyes of God

Today's readings are wonderful. The first comes from the First Book of Samuel and continues the narrative that we've heard proclaimed for a little more than the last week, first with the calling of Samuel by God and now his mission on God's behalf to anoint the new king. Found in the beginning of the sixteenth chapter, we hear how Samuel was sent to the house of Jesse who presented his sons, one by one, to Samuel. Each was impressive in his own right, apparently appearing regal and strong, but Samuel was told by God not to be distracted by appearances. We hear God's response to Samuel's inquiry about one of Jesse's sons and we realize that we are dealing with a way of viewing the world very unlike our usual quotidian experience:

"Do not judge from his appearance or from his lofty stature, because I have rejected him. Not as man sees does God see, because he sees the appearance but the LORD looks into the heart."

Not as human beings see does God see. This is so significant that we should not let the passage slip by us unacknowledged. The impact of this statement about how God operates gets lost so often amid the self-righteous and self-important promulgations and attitudes we human beings espouse.

Things that *seem* to make sense — like a strong young eldest son to be made king or the right to amass private wealth in our own day — only make sense to us according to our own rules. But how often do we pause to consider how *God sees* a given situation or decision?

This was Samuel's hang-up. He didn't realize how God saw the situation and what God intended in selecting David, the youngest and smallest and one overlooked by Jesse.

The way God sees has nothing to do with eyes at all. God "looks" into the hearts of all of us, knows what we *really* hold to be true, where our real priorities rest, how we really feel about others and God.

We live in an age fascinated with appearances and presentation, about looks and power, about money and 'success.' Yet, are these things important to God? If not, then why are they so important to us?

The lesson Samuel and Jesse (and, really, David) learn in the First Reading is a lesson that Jesus tries to teach his contemporary religious leaders in the Gospel: God is not at all concerned about the picky rules that human beings have created as an end in themselves instead of the means to God that the Lord intended. God does not see the exterior appearances about which we become obsessed. What is more important, Jesus asks, a focus on what food someone eats at what time and on what day? Or how that person lives *in relationship* to God, others and all creation?

Christians in general, but especially Roman Catholics, tend to become too much like the Pharisees in the Gospel, too much like Jesse in the Old Testament.

We live our lives by standards of our own making, playing

them off as "God's Law" (or "Natural Law" or "Divine Law" or "Canon Law" and so on).

We exclude others when we should include them; we condemn others when we should forgive them; we harm others when we should heal them; we judge others when we should embrace them; and we leave people in darkness when we should bring light to them.

The Wisdom that comes to us in Sacred Scripture today challenges us to see with the eyes of God and not with our own set of myopic lenses.

The world looks very differently when we try to look into the hearts of others as God does to us and not make our decisions based on appearances alone.

January 17, 2011

56

Political Splinters and Religious Planks

The liturgical season of Ordinary Time can really seem anything but ordinary when one looks at the powerful, challenging and important passages from Sacred Scripture that are proclaimed during these weekdays. In the last two weeks we've heard that we are to forgive, love our enemies, pray for and help usher in the Kingdom of God by doing God's Will, and today we are told "Stop judging" and "Why do you notice the splinter in your brother's eye, but do not perceive the wooden beam in your own eye?" (Matthew 7: 1-5). These are not easy readings, not easy commands and explanations for what it means to be a Christian in our world, but they are our instruction from the Lord no less.

The challenge of these Gospel passages reminds me of Ross Douthat's recent book, *Bad Religion: How We Became a Nation of Heretics* (Free Press, 2012). Although I don't always agree with the *New York Times* columnist — who admittedly is a Roman Catholic — I really like this book, at least I really appreciate his premise and efforts to contribute to a meaningful dialogue.

At the center of his project is addressing the question of the role of religion in our modern society and its relationship to the challenges or problems of our age: politically, socially, culturally and so on. He reminds us that there are two very popular, very polarizing perspectives that dominate the discussion. On the one hand you have the self-proclaimed "secular atheists" representing one extreme. These folks claim that religion has brought nothing but trouble and that religious zealots of our day are largely responsible for the ills of our society. On the other hand you have the so-called "Christian Right" and the particular brand of religious people that claims all our ills today are the result of the "increase of secularization" and that we don't have enough religion in the public square.

Douthat, however, argues that both sides are inherently wrong: we neither have *too much* nor *too little* religion. Instead, we have a lot of *bad religion!*

On this point, I tend to agree with Douthat. His point is that we've become heretics in the process of trying to live a "Christian life" by creating Christianity, oftentimes, in our own images and likenesses. Authentic Christianity then becomes replaced by the agendas and goals of many "conservative and liberal, political and pop cultural, traditionally religious and fashionably 'spiritual'" views. He goes on:

> That's where you'll find the reality of contemporary religion, and the roots of our present crisis. It's an America that remains the most religious country in the developed world, as God-besotted today as ever; a place where Jesus Christ is an obsession, God's favor a birthright, and spiritual knowledge an all-consuming goal. But it's also a place where traditional Christian teachings have been warped into justifications for solipsism and anti-intellectualism, jingoism and utopianism, selfishness and greed.

The readings of the Gospel lately have been a stark reminder that there is indeed lots of "bad religion" in our midst, what Douthat likes to call "pseudo-Christianities." The fact that so many self-proclaimed Christians think it perfectly reasonable not to forgive, to hate their enemies, to endorse or enable violence, the do their will instead of God's, and to self-righteously judge others without a sense of their own sinfulness and areas in need of work only aids Douthat's point.

This brings us to today's Gospel — a very challenging one right up there with loving one's enemies — about the splinters in others' eyes and the planks or beams in our own.

Jesus could not be more direct in this passage from Matthew: "Stop Judging" and "How can you say to your brother, 'Let me remove that splinter from your eye,' while the wooden beam is in your eye? You hypocrite, remove the wooden beam from your eye first; then you will see clearly to remove the splinter from your brother's eye."

I think this message speaks to us in two ways: (a) in a personal manner and (b) in a broader way that speaks to the whole Christian community.

Concerning the personal dimension of Jesus's admonition and instruction to us, it seems to me that so very often what annoys me about others or that about which I am most critical of others, when I'm most honest and reflective, tends to point toward something about me that is need of work or improvement. This could be the shared material that makes up both the splinter and plank, the common bond of wood that interferes with each of our abilities to see. Jesus is unequivocal when he says that I need to work on those things in my life first, be aware of my own sinfulness first, clear my own vision first — before I start judging and condemning others (the secret is: we are always in need of improvement and humility, so there won't be a point when I "can" judge and condemn others).

Not an easy thing to work on or do!

But there's also something of a corporate implication here for the entire Christian community collectively. We are oftentimes reminded in Scripture that Jesus was most critical of and vehement in his chastisements to religious leaders, those who professed to live their religious lives publicly and guide others in their respective spiritual journeys.

We have so many stark reminders today of the planks in the "Church's eye" — the recent conviction of a Philadelphia monsignor for his role in covering up the horrendous abuse of minors is a painful reminder of the many wooden beams the continue to blind the eyes of the corporate Body of Christ!

Similarly, there's a lot of talk lately of "religious freedom" and, subsequently, there has been raised the specter of infringement on this civil right by certain religious leaders. A very direct and significant editorial in the *Los Angeles Times,* the leading West-Coast Newspaper of record and the paper for the city and Archdiocese of the largest Catholic population in the United States, raises some serious concerns about the discussion of threats to religious freedom lately by religious leaders.

As a Christian community, particularly as Roman Catholics, we might not like to have such questions raised or challenges proffered to the ostensible teaching voice of our religious leaders, but then again we must remember that Jesus never let his own religious leaders off the hook — let us also not forget that in raising such questions and challenging such uses and abuses of power, he was crucified at their hands.

What the *Los Angeles Times* editorial, whether one agrees with the paper or not, invites us to consider is the true complexity of the circumstances and the seeming simplicity with which these questions have been handled by religious leaders and members of their faith communities. Who is infringing on whose religious liberty? Where is the threat originating? For whom is there even a threat?

Legal scholars, including leading Catholic lawyers and scholars, have respectfully, but sternly, challenged the pretext of the so-called "threat to religious liberty." Professor of Law and Theology, Cathleen Kaveny, of the University of Notre Dame, wrote:

> The bishops tend to frame their complaint in terms of religious liberty. Yet most religious-liberty cases involve minority religious groups seeking to be left alone to pursue holiness as they see fit, free from the baleful attention or coercion of the majority. They want to worship as they wish (*Church of Lukumi Babalu Aye v. City of Hialeah,* 1993) or educate their children as they think faith requires (*Wisconsin v.*

Yoder, 1972). Recognizing themselves as religious and moral minorities, most religious-liberty plaintiffs do not try to influence the broader community. Nor do they attempt to recast American society in their own image.

Yet, this is what is apparently happening today — religious leaders in the public square seek to "recast American society in their own image," to use Kaveny's phrase. In doing so, it would seem that the infringement on religious freedom isn't coming from a government interested in dictating how one is to practice his or her faith, but instead from a large faith community in this nation that wishes to impose a particular view of morality or practice on others, including those who are of a different denomination, faith tradition, or those of no affiliation at all. There is a lot here to think about and upon which to reflect.

Today's Gospel warns all Christians, and Jesus's constant focus on the responsibility and duties of religious leaders (*a fortiori* those leaders today who bear His name and claim to follow Him) makes this even more relevant for those in leadership and ministry, to be mindful of the need we have to first work on our weaknesses, sinfulness and ineptitude in terms of charity, forgiveness, peacemaking, love and justice!

It might strike some observers as though there is a political splinter that is the focus of some religious leaders who are blinded by the religious plank in their own eyes.

What does the Gospel in this extraordinary Ordinary Time tell us about what it means to live a Christian life in our contemporary society? If Jesus Christ were physically among us today as he was 2,000-years-ago, who would he chastise? Who would he embrace? And are we willing to finally do the same?

June 25, 2012

57

Life is not Fair... Thank God!

"That's not fair," someone might say.

"*Life* is not fair!" another person is likely to respond.

This little dialogue is something that is repeated in so many settings, from little children who aren't allowed to stay up as late as their older siblings to those employees tasked with working on Saturday after an already long week (*Office Space* anyone?). We are accustomed to hearing and saying "life is not fair" in order to justify or make sense of situations that seem unfair or unjust to us. It's usually a line invoked when someone is unable to get what he or she wants.

I'm not sure that is the best way, at least from a Christian vantage point, to understand and use the "life is not fair" truism. In fact, I'm pretty much convinced that it has extraordinarily positive connotations that have not been adequately considered.

For instance, take the way that God is portrayed in the Gospels. Perhaps the most striking example of God's lack of "fairness" comes in the parables that portray God as gratuitously generous and, dare I say, prodigal. Remember the passage about the wealthy landowner who hires laborers to tend his fields at various points during the day?

> "For the kingdom of heaven is like a landowner who went out early in the morning to hire men to work in his vineyard. He agreed to pay them a denarius for the day and sent them into his vineyard." About the third hour he went out and saw others standing in the marketplace doing nothing. He told them, 'You also go and work in my vineyard, and I will pay you whatever is right.' So they went.
>
> "He went out again about the sixth hour and the ninth hour and did the same thing. About the eleventh hour he went out and found still others

standing around..." He said to them, 'You also go and work in my vineyard.'" When evening came, the owner of the vineyard said to his foreman, 'Call the workers and pay them their wages, beginning with the last ones hired and going on to the first....' So when those came who were hired first, they expected to receive more. But each one of them also received a denarius. When they received it, they began to grumble against the landowner... he answered one of them, 'Friend, I am not being unfair to you. Didn't you agree to work for a denarius? Take your pay and go. I want to give the man who was hired last the same as I gave you. Don't I have the right to do what I want with my own money? Or are you envious because I am generous?'" So the last will be first, and the first will be last." (Matt 20:1-16)

Not very fair, at least by our culture's standards. Those who work more deserve to be paid more, right?

Or what about the story of the father with two sons? You may know it better as the parable of the "prodigal" (that is, lavishly spending, wastefully extravagant, etc.) son found in Luke 15:11-32. There's no need to rehearse it here, you know it. The younger son asks for his share of the inheritance (read: "Dad, I wish you were dead."), which the father gives him only to have it squandered by the heir on wasteful things. The son returns home, realizing that he would be better off treated as some servant of his father instead of living in the squalor conditions he brought upon himself (which would be, after, fair given how he treated his own father and then spent his share of the estate). But instead of subjecting him to the fair punishment of servitude, the father — much to the other son's chagrin — welcomes his youngest son home with love an celebration. The older son is furious and seemingly righteous in his indignation at how unfair the treatment of his brother seems.

Life is indeed not fair, that is what, in part, the message of Jesus was all about. Turning upside-down the expectations, standards and currency of judgment used by human prudence and society. Instead, God is a God of unprecedented unfairness... that is, by our standards.

The God of Jesus, the God of the Gospels, would not do well in a state that permitted capital punishment or did not provide healthcare and other resources for those without or sought revenge on the battlefield at home and abroad. No, this God would be radically unfair by the standards of the other son and the day laborers who felt "ripped off," not because of what was owed them and not given, but because of the generosity received by someone else entirely.

Life is not "fair" when all are treated as brothers and sisters deserving God's brand of justice and mercy, and not when the self-righteous flavor of "fairness" touted by the wealthy, the powerful, the "in-crowd," the majority and the rest comes to bear on those on the margins. This sense of unfairness is indeed only unfair to those who wish that others suffer or go without.

The sense that life is not fair according to the God of Scripture is actually much more *fair* and *just* than we can possibly conceive. Perhaps we need to act a little "less fairly" by worldly standards in order to act more justly in the eyes of God.

October 29, 2010

58

Death, Advent, and Hopeful Waiting

I must first express my sincere apologies to all of you regular readers who have been wondering where the daily (or near-daily) posts have been on *DatingGod.org* recently. As some of you might know, last week my family and I celebrated the life of my grandfather who entered into eternal life over the Thanksgiving holiday weekend. It was, as any death is, a challenging time, but a very blessed one as well. Just a few days ago one of my brother Franciscan friars with whom I lived here in Silver Spring, Harry Monaco, OFM, who was only in his late forties, also died. He had been struggling with a terminal form of cancer for several months and had been aware that his earthly pilgrimage was coming to an end, but didn't know that his *transitus* from this life to the next would happen so suddenly. We are still mourning our loss, making funeral and memorial arrangements, all the while preparing for the business of Christmas and the Advent season and finishing the academic semester on top of it all.

It is with the specter of death that has, in some sense, haunted these last few weeks that I reflect this morning on the meaning of Advent and the connection our faith has to the universal experience of our human finitude. I thought of Thomas Merton's little-known essay, "Advent: Hope or Delusion?" as I considered the meaning of death during the season of Advent. Merton begins his essay with the following thoughts:

> The certainty of Christian hope lies beyond passion and beyond knowledge. Therefore we must sometimes expect our hope to come in conflict with darkness, desperation and ignorance. Therefore, too, we must remember that Christian optimism is not a perpetual sense of euphoria, an indefectible comfort in whose presence neither anguish nor tragedy can possible exist. We must not strive to maintain a climate of optimism by the mere *suppression* of tragic realities. Christian optimism lies in a hope of victory that transcends all tragedy: a victory in which we *pass beyond* tragedy to glory with Christ crucified and risen (emphasis original).

It seems to me that this serves as a great starting point for some reflecting on Advent and Christian hope in the wake of death. As Franciscans we believe, following the wisdom and insight of Francis of Assisi who sought to live the Gospel, that death is not an end, nor is it a "beginning" as some people like to say (as if to suggest that what we live on earth is distinctly one thing, biding our time prior to "starting" the *real* life of heaven), but instead is a natural transition, or part of human existence.

Long before others will talk about the *existentials* of human existence — those aspects universally shared by all of humanity — Francis recognized in the *good news* (Gospel) of

Jesus Christ that death is not something to be feared nor something to be glorified, but something that is part of human reality that leads into something beyond. In his famous *Canticle of the Creatures*, Francis calls death our "Sister," a fundamental part of the created order. She, death that is, is something to be embraced because it is death that provides the condition for the possibility of eternal life with God.

Likewise, it is Jesus Christ who, as I like to say, "changed the game forever" when it comes to death. It is not the final word, it does not have the conclusive say, but is instead one part of our lifelong journey in relationship with God, others and all creation.

The Advent hope that Merton talks about urges us to confront head-on the challenges, darknesses, desperation and ignorance of our world, but to do so with the realization that they do not win out. Even death becomes subordinated to life in God. One of the things we are encouraged to consider is the way in which we as Christians hope to share in the victory over death and for life that Christ has won for us. That like Christ, we have been crucified in baptism and will share in Christ's Resurrection.

This was the last thing that my Franciscan brother Harry spoke with me about in this life. Sitting in his room a day and a half before he embraced Sister Death, we talked briefly about how he was doing. He shared his frustration that he no longer had the energy to stay awake long enough to read, something he enjoyed very much as an academic and a very contemplative person. But, he told me, when he does find enough energy to read a little, he reads short passages from Scripture — all of which are about the resurrection and eternal life. He knew that his time was coming to enter into the next life and he had tremendous faith in the resurrection, despite the pain and suffering he endured.

That his last words to me were about his certainty about the resurrection and that death was not the end will stay with me always. I pray that I might have just a small amount of the Advent Hope that he lived to the end, knowing that death is, as Francis reminds us, our Sister to embrace in our own time and recall that what the Incarnation (Christmas), death and resurrection (Easter) are all about is that death is not at all the end.

May we all, as the former translation of the Mass used to proclaim: "wait in joyful hope for the coming of our Savior, Jesus Christ."

December 7, 2011

59

Jesus Reminds Us of a God who Loves and Needs Us

Today's Gospel selection, the encounter of Jesus with the Samaritan woman at the well, is so rich and powerful that it has always been one of my most treasured images of who God is for us. In John's Gospel Jesus is always seen as the "one who makes God known," as the scripture scholar Francis Moloney puts it. The author of John's Gospel makes this abundantly clear in the Prologue to the Gospel where we learn that Jesus is not only the Word of God, but the exegesis of the God, the Symbol of the Father, the one who makes manifest who God is for us.

This past Christmas I preached at a parish in Utica, NY, about the significance of the celebration of the Incarnation, of Christmas, as a time for us to remember that God entered our world as one like us, dependent like us and in need like us. God's power, as St. Paul makes clear time and again, is not found in independence and earthly strength, but in humility and powerlessness that strikes listeners as foolishness and stupidity. That's our God, foolish and stupid…by *our standards,* of course.

This is yet another powerful Gospel encounter that reveals a glimpse into who God is. The details of this passage cannot be overlooked — as they often are — if you want to understand the fullness of what is transpiring between Jesus and the woman.

Take, for example, the seemingly gratuitous inclusion of the time of day. John's Gospel reads: "Jesus, tired from his journey, sat down there at the well. It was about noon." Who cares, right?

Well, it's important to know that no self-respecting woman would be strolling up to the well at noon by herself to collect water in that culture. Most of the women would have gone outside the inhabited part of town to gather water at the well at a much earlier time in the morning along with the other women. That this woman was by herself and going at a time when she wouldn't encounter anybody else bespeaks her social condition — she is shamed, pushed outside of the boundaries of normal community. She has done something wrong and has been forced to pay the price. She is a sinner and unclean.

Not only that, but she's a Samaritan. Remember that the reason the parable of the "Good Samaritan" was so powerful in Jesus's time was because it reversed the expected roles of the characters. This is one of two reasons that scholars suggest Jesus should never have been speaking to her: she's (a) a Samaritan and (b) a woman. His religious and cultural expectation would have been to ignore her.

The woman's response supports the scandal and irregularity of Jesus's request for water. She doesn't understand why a Jew would be asking for a drink from the same cup used by a Samaritan (and a sinful woman at that). Yet, Jesus is not phased by the religious and cultural expectations placed on him nor by the shock and confusion of the woman who rightly expected to be ignored or worse from this Jewish man.

What Jesus does is reveal his dependence. He has traveled all day (while the passage is often translated as noon, "midday" might be more accurate and its place in the Roman sense of time might place the encounter closer to 6:00pm than 12:00 noon) and is exhausted. His friends have gone off to find something to eat and left him to rest alone.

Before he offers the water of life, he offers himself over and against the expectation to withhold and remain independent, avoiding the unclean, sinful and unlovable woman. Yet, Jesus risks entering into relationship with the Samaritan woman with abandon. He expresses his dependence on her generosity and assistance, despite her place in society, despite her shame and sin, despite her weakness.

How great a love! Jesus does not get tangled up in the battles of condemnation and shame. He is not concerned about the legalistic interpretation of the Law that would forbid him from talking — let alone sharing a cup — with the woman. God's love transcends the limitations we put on each other. God's love is not restricted to the righteous or upstanding, it's not reserved for the overtly religious or even the professed believers, God's love is for *all* — especially those who are the least loveable.

If God can so freely reveal an openness to relationship and express dependence on those who we push to the margins of our own society, why can't we? The Samaritan woman was an adulterer and someone outside of Jesus's own religion, yet he picks her to enter into relationship with, share who he is and ask for something that only she at that time can give.

If only we could do the same as readily. Jesus reminds us not only of God's overabundant love for *all* people — righteous and sinner, Christian and non-Christian alike — but models for us how God expects US to live. We are to be Christ for one another, reaching out to others in love, sharing our human dependence and embracing those we are expected to despise.

March 27, 2011

60

Not Letting the Tail Wag the Dog, or Why I Readily Admit to Being a Bad Christian

To be honest, I must admit, like all followers of Christ, I am an imperfect Christian.

I struggle daily — as I expect I will for the entirety of my life — to live following the Gospel and frequently fall short of where God is calling me to be. I mention this seemingly obvious fact because I think its admittance is what hinders so many from authentically advocating and striving toward the fullest meaning of Christian life.

What I mean by this is that, in fear of coming across as hypocritical (I am convinced that no finite person can do otherwise now and then, even the saints exhibit lives of at-times contradiction), so many end up creating the Gospel in their own image and likeness. Or, what is more likely, gloss over certain mandates that compel men and women who bear the name Christ to act, speak, and serve in certain ways that they would otherwise prefer not to do.

Take, for example, the recent conversation surrounding the admittance of the Governor of New York to the Eucharistic table by the Bishop of Albany in January. Seeking to decry certain public forms of sin, many (including a prominent canonist and blogger) have spoken out against the bishop's action, suggesting that the proper course of action is to forbid this or that person (especially democratic governors) from the Table of the Lord.

Yet, the example of Jesus — whom, lest we forget, Christians believe is the decisive embodiment of God's Revelation – demonstrates, without contrast, that it was precisely the sinners and publicans who were first in line to break bread with the Lord. Scholars have time and again called our attention to the central role table fellowship had for the public ministry of Jesus and it was rarely with the pristine of repute and sinless in the popular conceptualization.

On the contrary, it was the least among society, the forgotten, the abused, the marginalized, the poor and unclean, the nobodies and the public sinners that — according to law and popular sentiment — deserved to be stoned.

I have the most difficult time living up to my Baptismal commitment to live as a member of the Body of Christ, because to do so requires doing things and acting in a way that is counterintuitive, selfless and charitable when what I normally want to do is so natural, selfish and unkind.

My guess is that this is also the case with so many who judge and condemn this or that public or political figure without much consideration for the scandal that Christ calls us to live. The justification invoked for the exclusion of some to the table is more often than not scandal, yet it was Christ who so scandalized the self-righteous that he was executed.

The scandal of Christ did not begin on the Cross, but led to it. The scandal of Christ is that while the self-righteous twist their arms patting themselves on the back and celebrating the laudable accomplishments of this or that public condemnation, Christ sits among the condemned and unwanted, embracing the sinner as only God can.

God favors the poor, the lost, the forgotten. Scripture, apart from proof-texting contextual-less passages, does not legitimize that which is so often endorsed by popular imagination at the expense of others. Scripture reveals that God is not a God who favors the powerful, wealthy and members of the in-crowd, but subjects Himself to their taunts, bears the brunt of their abuse and endures the piercing pain of their nails for the sake of those so many wish to exclude from the celebration of thanksgiving (*eucharistia*) for precisely this gift of God's love.

I am willing to admit that I am a bad Christian, an imperfect follower of the Word-Made-Flesh because it allows me to stand for what I strive to live more perfectly: the Gospel. It strikes me as a sign of the self-righteous that they knock others down with an aim to minimize the Church, which is the Body of Christ with all its members, in order to justify their own need to feel acceptable or even superior.

Conversion is a life-long process and being a Christian requires the surrendering one's entire life. It happens in little steps, with little decisions and actions. While I continue to be an imperfect Christian, I strive toward living more perfectly that way of life that God in God's own example modeled for us in Jesus Christ. I refuse to let others dictate who is and who is not welcome when I know that God welcomes all. I only hope that I can become more welcoming, more Christ-like in this life. My prayer is that we might all do so.

March 1, 2011

PART 5

POLITICS AND RELIGION
IN THE PUBLIC SQUARE

61

The Eucharist is not a Weapon: Part I

The Celebration of the Eucharist is not a Game

It's fair to say that St. Francis of Assisi understood the celebration of the Eucharist to be the center of his entire spiritual life. For the thirteenth-century saint, few subjects appear as frequently (perhaps it is only the Gospel that appears more regularly) as the Blessed Sacrament in his writings and personal reflections. Some of the most powerful prayers the saint penned, while they've been frequently overlooked by most Christians and remain largely unknown, come from his meditation on the Sacramental presence of Christ in the Eucharist. And as someone who has committed his life to following in the footprints of Francis of Assisi, seeking to life the Gospel after his example, I think it's important to discuss the importance of the Eucharist and certain contemporary issues related to it.

For Francis, the Eucharist was so important that nothing could come between him and his participation in the liturgical celebration. Likewise, nothing should come between any member of the faithful and the Blessed Sacrament; Including, and most importantly, priests, bishops, or any minister of Communion.

This might sound odd to those who are familiar with the all-too-common "Communion wars" that have broken out in various dioceses of the United States in recent year, usually around election season. The situation is likely familiar to many of you, Catholic or not. Some politician (usually a democrat) is declared to be unworthy to receive Holy Communion in a given Catholic diocese. The usual charge is one's political affiliation with positions relating to abortion (almost no other issue attracts such attention). However, one recent example in the diocese where I currently reside has garnered significant attention and, for once, is not directly related to a political stance on abortion rights.

Why Bishop Hubbard was 100% Correct

The incident took place here in Albany, NY, last month on the day after Andrew Cuomo was inaugurated as Governor of New York. Cuomo attended the Cathedral in Albany for Sunday Mass with his girlfriend and some members of his family. Bishop Howard Hubbard of Albany was the Celebrant and has since come under fire from certain commentators for distributing Communion to Cuomo who is currently living with his unwed girlfriend. The Albany newspaper *The Times-Union* explains:

> A consultant for the Vatican's high court says he believes New York Gov. Andrew Cuomo shouldn't receive the Catholic sacrament of Holy Communion because he is not married to his live-in girlfriend, Food Network star Sandra Lee.
>
> Edward Peters, who's also a conservative Catholic blogger and seminary professor in Detroit, called the living arrangement "public concubinage" and said that Cuomo taking Communion would be sacrilegious.

Bishop Hubbard responded in, what I believe, is one of the best responses someone in his position could have given. Here is what he is quoted as saying in another *Times-Union* article:

> Albany Bishop Howard Hubbard says it is "unfair and imprudent" to conclude that Gov. Andrew Cuomo and his girlfriend, Sandra Lee, shouldn't receive communion simply because they're living together.
>
> "There are norms of the church governing the sacraments, which Catholics are expected to observe,"
>
> Hubbard wrote in a brief statement. "However, it is unfair and imprudent to make a pastoral judgment about a particular situation without knowing all the facts.

"As a matter of pastoral practice we would not comment publicly on anything which should be addressed privately, regardless if the person is a public figure or a private citizen," Hubbard wrote in conclusion.

Perhaps one of the most significant problems with Edward Peters's position is the presumption necessary to justify denial of Holy Communion. To say that someone is unworthy to participate fully in the Celebration of the Eucharist is a very bold claim, one that I and others would argue no person can make without explicit and public demonstration at the time of reception that demonstrates one's lack of proper disposition — a very rare occurrence, that can almost never be substantiated.

The only person that can know the state of someone's soul (as the language goes) is the individual person and, perhaps, his or her confessor. But the confessor is, under the threat of excommunication, forbidden from disclosing or acting on that knowledge. So no minister of Communion — ordinary or "extraordinary" — is in any justifiable position to refuse a member of the faithful who presents him or herself at the Celebration of the Eucharist to receive Holy Communion. Period.

Stop Using The Eucharist as a Weapon

Presumption of the condition of this or that person's "soul" or, more accurately, their relationship with God and the rest of the Body of Christ, is something that is necessary to make any public statement calling for ministers to withhold Communion from others.

In the recent case involving Gov. Cuomo, the presumption is one of a sexual nature. See, in order for there to be a problem, the minister of Communion would have to know that the Governor and his girlfriend are engaging in sexual intercourse outside of marriage *and* that he had not participated in the Sacrament of Reconciliation prior to the Celebration of the Eucharist. One cannot know that information about another. As Bishop Hubbard said, "it is unfair and imprudent to make a pastoral judgment about a particular situation without knowing all the facts."

Staying with this case for a minute, the arrogance of Peters and others who make such bold and unjust claims calling for other members of the faithful to be denied Sacramental participation in the Eucharist is staggering. There are millions of example of co-habitation that do not necessarily evoke presumptive opinions about sexual misbehavior. Think of college roommates. As I said last night to our campus chaplain here at this Catholic college, if we were to follow Peters's approach, no student who lived in the dorms with another person could rightfully be admitted to Communion. They are not only living together, but sharing a room. And by Peters's standards, we *must* presume they are engaging in some sort of sexual behavior.

I don't know about you, but when I was in college that was certainly not the case. I lived in the dorms and then in on-campus upperclassmen apartments with roommates and we never found ourselves in such a "state of sin." Yet, that is, technically and practically speaking, the operative lens in Peters's and others' assessment. Similarly, I currently live with more than twenty other non-married men. We are professed religious, Franciscan friars, but none of us are married and we share the same address. Does Peters presume that all nuns, friars, religious or diocesan priests who reside together are engaging in sexual misbehavior? Granted, we friars have our own rooms yet live in the same house, but what is to make me believe that Cuomo and Lee don't have a comparable living arrangement? Assumption and stereotype is *what*. And that is all.

The treatment of certain political figures in this fashion reveals less of a theological or even moral concern than it does an opportunity to wield a wholly (and Holy) inappropriate weapon against a political opponent. This sort of action needs to stop.

Likewise, the matter is precisely the same in the case of so-called "pro-choice" candidates and their respective harassment by fellow Catholics. We simply cannot judge the state of another person's soul, nor know the complexities of lives — spiritual, political or otherwise. What is there to say that there isn't a matter of Canonical Internal Forum, a case of recent participation in the Sacrament of Reconciliation or myriad other possibilities that the self-righteous and presumptive protesters never consider?

In such cases the Eucharist becomes a weapon and laymen like Edward Peters and Bishops like those who appear in the news during the election cycle who call for denying Holy Communion and full participation in the Celebration of the Eucharist to political figures are the ones acting unjustly and causing scandal (lit: "stumbling block" from the Greek *skandalon*) to the faithful. Who did Jesus refuse at table? The sinner or the self-righteous?

This must stop.

February 25, 2011

62

The Eucharist is not a Weapon: Part II

Those who have been waiting for the second installment of the "The Eucharist is not a Weapon" post from earlier this year can rest easy now that another Eucharist-related conflict has necessitated this particular post. The matter this time doesn't have to do with a politician receiving Holy Communion (for once), but instead we are witnessing something much more insidious and seemingly innocuous — a couple of United States bishops restricting the distribution of Holy Communion under both species (bread *and* wine) to the faithful, reserving it only for the most limited instances prescribed by the rubrics, namely to the priest and deacon alone unless there is some special celebration.

The argument for this move, at least as it is presented in the Dioceses of Madison, WI, recently (here is the full text of the cathedral bulletin where this news was first published) and Phoenix, AZ, is that the expiration of a Vatican Indult in 2005 ostensibly concerning the distribution of Communion under both species. However, a record of this alleged Indult is not easily acquired. What can be found are a number of other

Indults near the same time: The permission for extraordinary ministers of the Eucharist to purify sacred vessels (1975, which is said to 'expire' in 2005) and the person to give communion to the faithful in-the-hand (1969 universally, 1979 in the US particularly), for example.

It is this first matter, the purification of sacred vessels, that seems to be the *real* legal argument that the bishop of Madison, bishop of Phoenix and perhaps some others are using for their squashing of Communion under both kinds. That is the so-called expired Indult and the matter, as it was explained in a 2006 CNS article on the subject, that Cardinal Arinze of the Congregation for Divine Worship stressed when the vessel-purification Indult "ran out." [For the full-text of the 2002 three-year extension of that Indult, accompanied by then USCCB President Archbishop Gregory's introduction, see here.]

Noting that the General Instruction of the Roman Missal "directs that the sacred vessels are to be purified by the priest, the deacon or an instituted acolyte," the cardinal said in his Oct. 12 letter that "it does not seem feasible, therefore, for the congregation to grant the requested indult from this directive in the general law of the Latin Church."

Although receiving Communion under both kinds is a "more complete" sign of the sacrament's meaning, Cardinal Arinze said, "Christ is fully present under each of the species."

How quickly the argument goes from a matter concerning which person can or cannot clean a chalice to the widespread denial of Communion under both kinds to thousands, or even millions, of the faithful.

It would appear that the Congregation for Divine Worship used this expiration as an opportunity to circumvent the directives of the *General Instruction of the Roman Missal (GIRM)*, which in its 2002 revised form reads:

> Holy Communion has a fuller form as a sign when it is distributed under both kinds. For in this form the sign of the eucharistic banquet is more clearly evident and clear expression is given to the divine will by which the new and eternal Covenant is ratified in the Blood of the Lord, as also the

relationship between the Eucharistic banquet and the eschatological banquet in the Father's Kingdom.

The *GIRM* also outlines what authority the local ordinary has in matters relating to Holy Communion under both kinds:

> The Diocesan Bishop may establish norms for Communion under both kinds for his own diocese, which are also to be observed in churches of religious and at celebrations with small groups. The Diocesan Bishop is also given the faculty to permit Communion under both kinds whenever it may seem appropriate to the priest to whom, as its own shepherd, a community has been entrusted, provided that the faithful have been well instructed and there is no danger of profanation of the Sacrament or of the rite's becoming difficult because of the large number of participants or some other reason.

Canon Law is notably silent on this matter as it directs pastors, clergy and the faithful to the liturgical laws of the Church (i.e., in this case, the *GIRM!*).

> Holy communion is to be given under the form of bread alone or under both species *according to the norm of the liturgical laws*, or even under the form of wine alone in the case of necessity. (Can. 925, *emphasis added*)

This whole business is very curious. It seems absurd that bishops, including the Prefect for the Congregation for Divine Worship in Rome, would be so myopic and concerned about this technicality ordering who is and who is not *fit to clean* the sacred vessels, objects which only contained the precious species, when the same faithful — extraordinary ministers of the Eucharist or otherwise — have already handled and consumed Holy Communion. In other words, they are fit to receive, handle and distribute Communion, but are not fit to purify a chalice (which, for those who don't know, consists of consuming the remaining particles of the Eucharist — which any baptized person is permitted to do according to the law, pouring water into the empty vessel, consuming that poured water, and drying the vessel itself with a purificator).

That the bishops of Phoenix and Madison, and anyone who in the future tries to use a similar justification for curbing access to Holy Communion under both species, are using this purification-of-vessels matter as the rationalization for restricting or refusing the Eucharist is a scandal in itself. The faithful have a right (according to Can. 912: "Any baptized person not prohibited by law can and must be admitted to holy communion") to receive Communion and this right, according to the liturgical law (*GIRM*, etc.) leans toward communion under both species as normative unless it becomes impossible due to circumstances such as large numbers of people or lack of access to wine.

Here we come to the title of this post: The Eucharist is Not a Weapon.

It strikes me as nothing less-than an clerical overstepping and unnecessary demarcation of the clergy and laity. What are these pastors (by which I mean the Canonical notion of pastor) thinking? It seems, at least superficially, that it is an "in" and "out" club — who is and who is not permitted to receive from the cup. The only shred of juridical support is the technicality about who can and cannot clean the cups after Communion. Seriously, we have more important things to be concerned about. Provided the extraordinary ministers of the Eucharist, with some very simple instruction and supervision of the presider, know what they are doing and are respectful — as the law demands — of their duty, then there should be absolutely no problem with their purification of the sacred vessels.

It is, one must admit, rather humorous that these men are so very concerned about who "does the dishes," as it were. If only the married women who are oftentimes the extraordinary ministers of the Eucharist could instill such a fervent desire in their husbands at home, there might be fewer fights between couples in the kitchen after dinner!

October 10, 2011

63

"Losing my Religion": A Tale of American Christianity

I have become somewhat convinced, although I'm still working out the implications and sources of what I'm about to posit, that the rise of the so-called 'Christian Right' in recent decades concurrently caused the loss of authentic religious identity in many of the Christian communities in the United States.

What, you might ask, are you talking about? Hear me out.

In preparation for teaching a seminar this afternoon, I had been doing a lot of reading about the experience of faith and religion as it relates to Christianity in the United States. Among the different texts and narratives I've been studying up on, there is included a cast of evangelical Christians of sound academic reputation, including: Mark Noll (Notre Dame), Randall Balmer (Columbia), Alan Wolfe (Boston College), among others.

A common theme that arose in each thinker's reflection is the phenomenon of so-called "megachurches" that have sprouted up around the U.S. in recent decades. Alan Wolfe, in the book *The Life of Meaning* (2007), explains:

> The whole megachurch phenomenon is premised upon the idea that we can't do anything with people unless we get them to church first, so the priority is to get them in there. But to get them in there, you downplay the Christian symbolism, you take the crosses off the church, you make the pews as comfortable as you possible can, you put McDonald's franchises in the lobby. Sometimes you don't even know you're in church when you go to church, because the church doesn't look like a church.

> It's clear that that's what the people want. If you're in the business of getting the people there, you've got to give them what they want. But it comes at a huge cost. They call themselves evangelical, but they're not

strict, not demanding. Willow Creek, the most
famous of our megachurches, doesn't even have a
cross outside the building. It won't identify itself with
any specific tradition. It wants to grow. And the way
you grow is by trying to be all things to all people.

To be fair, I would suggest that it's not just an evangelical
issue. Lots of other Christian communities find themselves in
a similar cycle.

Nobody is going to church → you want people to go
to church → they'll go if it was less-like-church →
you make it less-like-church → the substance and
content becomes lost, because the context has
changed.

If you are audience-driven, you cannot challenge or raise
questions the hearer hasn't asked or wants to hear. Instead of
throwing seed down in hope of it finding fertile soil, you ditch
the whole seeding effort leaving the land to remain rocky and
infertile.

So where's the Gospel?

Balmer believes that the rise of the 'Religious Right' was
one small group's attempt to make a certain type of
evangelical Christianity, a narrowly conceived form of
Christianity, the "hegemonic expression of faith for the entire
culture" of the United States.

The problem, as I see it, is that with the dissolution of the
churches' message as one of substance and Gospel-inspired
content, those who find it fashionable to maintain the
descriptor "Christian" needed another signifying focus — if
church and my religion no longer resemble authentic
Christianity, then I need to replace it with something I can
choose to identify as explicitly "Christian."

Witness the emergence of a morality-based political
rhetoric that both implicitly and expressly identifies certain
hot-button "moral" issues as necessary foci for Christians in
the public and political squares. How do you know that so-
and-so is a Christian? Because he or she is "prolife" or "anti-
same-sex-marriage," or something of the sort. Meanwhile, this
person goes to "church" on Sunday, is told what he or she

wants to hear, gives money to the pastor, sings a few upbeat songs, and goes home righteous as ever.

As the authentic Christian identity of ecclesial communities dissolves in an effort to draw people and amass a veritable stadium of singing "new-christians," the political agenda of some has filled the vacuum of religious identity left vacant by the eclipse of the Gospel.

The thing about abortion and same-sex-marriage, to pick two of several contentious issues, is that they rarely impact the person rallying against them directly. On the other hand, the Gospel raises challenges for all people in every age and at all times. You can demonize the unwed and poor pregnant woman outside a Planned Parenthood office because you are not that person.

But we are *all* the Body of Christ, to whom God demands much for much has been given to us — more is demanded than political lip-service and vacuous religious affectivity. Unlike the targets of these political hot-button issues, the poor, the marginalized (who may also be your political targets), the forgotten and abused, they implicate all of us in a world that remains unjust.

When Christians become convinced that social justice is antithetical to Christian living, they have indeed lost their religion, replacing Christianity for vacuous political ideology. A sad tale of American Christianity indeed.

February 9, 2011

64

Christopher Hitchens and Death "Without God"

I have been doing a lot of reflecting on the mystery of death these last few weeks as the death of my grandfather one week was followed by the death of a young friar who lives in my community the next. As the title of Ernest Becker's classic text suggests, *The Denial of Death*, we as a species and, even more acutely, as a North American culture, like to live our lives in the denial of our ultimate earthly fate. News of the death of the infamous "new atheist" Christopher Hitchens yesterday has returned me to some of these timely reflections, recalling as I do what has struck me so powerfully in the experiences of the *transitus* – the "passing over" from this life to the next — of two people of faith, each in their own way. It was the meaning, individually and communally, that stayed with me, comforts me and brings a peace that helps calm the nerves of yet another person who will someday meet death, whom Francis of Assisi called "Sister."

In the moments before the procession began in which I and my family's local pastor would meet the body of my grandfather and rest of the family at the entrance of our parish church, I turned to Fr. Joe and said, "I have no idea how somebody without faith in the resurrection, without belief in God, without the Rites of the Church could make sense of what we celebrate here."

One thing that I came to appreciate in a very personal way during those last days of my grandfather's life in this world was the way in which our community of faith, the Church, marks the final moments of our life and celebrates that knowledge we possess in Christ's Resurrection that, through baptism, each of us also shares. There are prayers for illness, prayers for the moments of death, prayers after death. There are rituals of the "office of the dead," to be celebrated by religious and clergy in lieu of the usual cycle of daily prayers, and Masses offered in the memory of the deceased. There are Rituals for the wake service during which the family gathers with friends in prayer, prayers for the transferal of the body from the funeral home to the Church, a Mass of Christian Burial that is a celebration of Resurrection and Eternal Life more than a eulogy of a life finished, and a Rite for the committal of the body of the deceased in the place of rest.

Each of these moments mark a period of mourning, of sorrow, of celebration, of death, of life. Each of these moments always points to the mystery of the Resurrection and of Eternal Life.

But what does a militant and self-proclaimed atheist have?

I don't know. But I imagine that death for such people brings with it a fear that might not be found as acutely in the experience of those who prepare for a transition and not an end, who know of the love of God instead of the abandonment of fate, who are connected to the ground of their existence and not of the view that they are random iterations of matter.

I am not at all joyful in the death of Hitchens, nor do I wish he suffered any pain. In fact, I hope that his passage from this life to the next was as peaceful as possible. At the risk of sounding condescending or patronizing, I admit that I felt sorry for him. My sympathy does not arise from a victorious view of my own vindication, trusting as I do that he was quite surprised at the moment of his own death. My sympathy stems from the knowledge of what my faith has and continues to mean to me and billions of others on the planet that recognize that our existence, made more comprehensible by the advances of science, is in fact more than the sum of our parts and that there is more to existence than merely *existing*.

I am sorry that Hitchens did not allow himself to be swept away by the love of God made manifest in the world around him in a way that he could name it as such. But I am nevertheless convinced that he did experience that love of God.

As Karl Rahner makes clear in his own eschatological reflections, we are always and everywhere in relationship with God by virtue of our being lovingly created, in grace, in this world. However, God so loves us that we are given the constitutive character of freedom to reject that love and transcendental experience, taking responsibility (or shirking it) as we so choose.

Although Hitchens did not believe in God, I have no doubt that God most certainly believed in Hitchens. At least now he knows that.

December 16, 2011

65

Jesus Never Chastised the Poor, but He would have a Problem with Politicians and Wealthy Americans!

Contrary to the somewhat popular conservative narrative in contemporary United States politics, never do you find Jesus warning the poor of their lazy, foolish, abhorrent and reproachable ways. Yet, this is how those who are continually marginalized in our society, often for reasons far beyond their control, are depicted in some contemporary political rhetoric. I have grown absolutely sick of it.

When does Jesus get riled up? When is Jesus pissed off? It's when the business people take advantage of others, it's when the religious leaders burden the faithful, it's when the would-be disciples come up with half-hearted excuses about why that can't follow Him ("I have to bury my father," "I have to do this or that," and so on), it's when the *wealthy* walk away from discipleship sad because they cannot part with their belongings and greed.

> "Woe to you who are rich, for you have received your consolation. Woe to you who are full now for you will be hungry. Woe to you who are laughing now, for you will mourn and weep!" (Luke 6:24-25).

As I have mentioned earlier this week, my exposure to current news media is limited because of my month-long Solemn Vow retreat, but I do get snippets here and there. One thing that I have been following from a distance is the congressional and executive discussions about the US debt ceiling and the political jockeying that has been taking place under that heading. I have become increasingly frustrated with all sides, but particularly with those who are defending the ridiculously low tax rates for the most wealthy in our society, while jeopardizing the livelihood and security of the most vulnerable.

Jesus never had a problem with the poor. Yet these so-called "Christians" who tout their faith in campaign stump speeches, yet decry basic healthcare, financial and other services for the poor, seem convinced (and likewise seek to convince their constituents) that Jesus would support their political positions, which simply amount to protecting the private assets of the wealthiest while placing the burden of supporting the society on the shoulders of those who have less and less.

Those entirely out of touch with reality, the likes of Rep. Michelle Bachmann, are reported (the July 13 *Washington Post*) yesterday as saying that they welcome the financial collapse. For what purpose? To what end? The Catholic Church has been very clear in its 100+ years of social teaching that the purpose of a government is to protect the basic rights of its citizens, not secure a plutocracy for the few wealthiest among us.

For those who find the Lord's Sermon on the Mount not quite satisfactory and want (as so many who comment here and elsewhere online) some catechetical documentation, I will do something I so rarely do: reference the Catechism (which is a fine document for instructing catechumens or candidates for reception in the Church, which is what a *Catechism* is for! It is not for theological discussion nor is it intended to be a reference book of definitive authority).

> No. 2445: "Love for the poor is incompatible with immoderate love of riches or their selfish use."

> No. 2446: "St. John Chrysostom vigorously recalls this: 'Not to enable the poor to share in our goods is to steal from them and deprive them of life. The goods we possess are not ours, but theirs.' 'The demands of justice must be satisfied first of all; that which is already due in justice is not to be offered as a gift of charity.' When we attend to the needs of those in want, we give them what is theirs, not ours. More than performing works of mercy, we are paying a debt of justice."

For those who haven't picked up on the more

contemporary theme, what St. John is saying is what was echoed by Servant of God Dorothy Day and even the philosopher Peter Singer have said in our own time: anything you have beyond your *necessity* is stealing from the poor.

This is something of which I am certainly guilty. There are many things that I have or use that are simply not necessary. Three pairs of pants instead of two? How many books? You can imagine the ways in which we can quickly find so much that we appropriate that could otherwise serve the *needs* and not simply the *wants* of those who go without. All we have to do is pause and reflect.

But, it's much easier to believe and repeat the deceitful narratives that portray the wealthy as virtuous, "true, hardworking Americans," worthy of their excesses and luxury, while the poor deserve their misfortune, their destitution and their life. Where does this come from? This is not *Christian!* Can anyone tell me where in the Scriptures this is supported? Can someone show me a substantial theological text that buttresses this disturbed cosmology and ethics?

The wealthy and the greedy plant these seeds of self-justification in the minds of the lower classes and nurture the foul plant's growth with the fertilizer of their lies. They, in the meantime, remain unaffected by the turmoil of the economy, while those who continue to vote against themselves legislatively and otherwise suffer the downfall, all the while believing the mythic-scapegoat tales that the poor and working classes are to blame for the financial problems.

Do not raise the debt ceiling. That will only project more problems into the future. Instead, raise the taxes with the wealthiest first, charging those that can afford it first. Lest we forget that many of those who made off the best in recent years were also largely responsible for the economic downfall spurred on by greed and selfishness.

We cannot forget, as people of faith, of our responsibility to respond to systemic sin. The way our society continues to deal with its financial obligations to protect all people has really become sinful. The poor and the working class are who suffer, while the wealthy do just fine. If the Gospel is any indication of how Jesus would respond today, he would not chastise the poor, but he would have a serious problem with the politicians and their selfish behaviors at the expense of the lives of others. I could just see the Lord turning over tables in the House and Senate.

July 14, 2011

66

Christianity, the Poor, and the U.S. Debt Ceiling

I've been intentionally quiet about this issue for some weeks now. My reservation about commenting stems mostly from my uncertainty about how to respond to what I have seen as the continued exercise of injustice on the systemic level, while at the same time recognizing the short-term threat of not raising the US debt ceiling — something, it should be again noted, that has happened 78 times since 1962: 49 times by Republican administrations and 28 times be Democratic administrations. On one hand I think that this continued raising of the debt ceiling, a necessity born out of the continued spending beyond the federal revenue, is not helpful for long-term fiscal stability. Yet, it's immediate need is, in fact, non-negotiable.

The solution to this? In part, it's raising taxes on the most wealthy and on corporations. To *not* do so in association with any other form of response to the fiscal crunch *is irresponsible*, yet this is precisely what is being lobbied by the self-titled "Tea Partiers" in the GOP caucus. And, much to my chagrin, their hard-headed holdout seems to have paid-off for their agenda. As Fareed Zakaria has sagaciously pointed out, the creation of a "debt-ceiling crisis" is really the product of this small group's efforts to advance their own uniquely partisan interests — maintaining or increasing tax cuts for the wealthy and corporations. Such controversy surrounding the raising of the debt ceiling is particularly specious given the GOP's record of raising the limit nearly twice as often over the last several decades.

What is absolutely absurd about all of this is the trap into which the majority of legislators and government administrators have been lured. The concessions offered by the Democrats seem to have "sold out" the least among us, a clear sacrifice of the poorest and most vulnerable, while the GOP "Tea Partiers" gave little or no ground on their adamant defense of "no taxes." If the debt ceiling is such a pressing issue because our spending exceeds our federal revenue, then in addition to cutting expenditures (which I am in favor of, particularly that of the defense/military budget!!!!) the government should be able to collect the funds necessary to provide a safe and secure society for its citizens, which is not simply a cry to arms, but the providing of basic resources all humans need to live with dignity (i.e., the so-called "entitlements" that Republicans have decried. "Entitlements" like food, shelter and healthcare — indeed all human beings ARE "entitled" to those things).

As Christians, we have a particularly explicit mandate to speak up about matters and in times like these. The Gospel makes it very, very clear what we are to do in following God and in living in right relationship with one another. Jesus had *nothing* to say about abortion (something practiced in his time in Hellenistic and other contemporaneous cultures), nor did he say anything about "one's right to bear arms" (another 'biggy' among self-described "conservative Christians" in this country), but Jesus *did* have a lot to say about how the poor were to be treated. In fact, the Gospel of Matthew ends with perhaps the most famous and most overt account of Jesus's teaching on the matter, leading me to ask where do you and I stand: among the sheep or the goats? (Check out Matthew 25 if you don't know what I mean).

The *Washington Post* recently reported that minorities in this country, Latinos and African Americans, have and will suffer the most from the economic crises of the day. The economic imbalance in this country is absolutely staggering, as the *Post* reports:

> There is a racial component to the politics of social justice today. A recent report showed that from 2005-2009, Hispanics were the most affected by the Great Recession, losing more than half, that is, 66 percent of all we own. African Americans, who had

less to begin with, lost 53 percent of their wealth. But white Americans saw a drop of only 16 percent in their wealth. A Pew research team reported: "Median wealth of whites is now 20 times that of black households and 18 times that of Hispanic households, double the already marked disparities that had prevailed in the decades before the recent recession." Such economic imbalance, combative politics and racial inequality, has been the recipe for revolution in Third World countries, but is has now arrived in America. Catholic America needs to provide a living example of how to resist these temptations to class warfare and racial antagonism.

In the same article, the author, writing about the so-called Catholic response to the debt crisis, keenly writes:

Sadly, some bishops in the United States today seem to have fallen into the same trap by supporting Republican promises on abortion and same-sex marriage while ignoring the GOP's recent complicity in social engineering to benefit the super-wealthy.

The Catholic response is very, very clear. While abortion, torture, war and the like are indeed social injustices that must be decried, we cannot lose sight of the commandment set out by the Good News, that is *The Gospel*, to serve "the least among us." Anything less than that is a sin.

I think that the poor and working classes have suffered enough in these recent years, but how have the wealthy, the super-wealthy and the business sector contributed to alleviating the abject poverty, material suffering and social imbalance in our society? Answer: they haven't. The ruse that businesses or the wealthy "create jobs" and therefore deserve all sorts of unjust breaks while the poor labor on unceasingly and without reward is bullshit. Any legitimate economist will tell you that "job creation" is a much more complicated and nuanced than the stump-speech one-liners like that above imply. But, most people, I surmise, do not read or listen or discuss the detailed analyses of such subtle systems. Instead, it is the sound-bite delivery of distortion that informs too many.

If the deal to raise the debt ceiling that will be voted on today cuts services to the poor and marginalizes without comparatively affecting the wealthy, then this purported solution is a sham, a sin and a crime against humanity.

August 1, 2011

67

Changing Discourse:
The Lesson of Norway for the United States

The citizens of the global human family, but especially the Norwegians, continue to grapple with the tragedy of violence that struck the otherwise peaceful nordic land. When one thinks of violent religious extremism — "terrorism" is another word used by many commentators — one usually does not think of the face of a 32-year-old Scandinavian self-described Christian. And perhaps, I would argue, this is precisely part of the problem and, if you would allow me to be so bold without mistaking my comments, this is also part of what might contribute to the establishment of the condition for the possibility of such terror in an otherwise un-tumultuous society.

Let me explain.

I have said for some time now, perhaps in intermittent fashion and maybe without enough force, that the way in which certain people in the United States (and elsewhere) talk about people of other ethnicities, nationalities, religions, sexual orientations, genders or cultures promotes a rhetorical atmosphere of semantic violence. Words are incredibly powerful (see my comments after January's horrible attack on Rep. Giffords: "The Violent Power of Words: A Franciscan's Response"). There is sound reason to correlate the tone and tenor of public discourse about a minority population and the affect it has in shaping concrete actions. Any scholar of twentieth-century anti-semitism can attest to the veracity of such a claim.

With this in mind, I think that the primary lesson that this tragic experience in Norway presents to the rest of the world is an opportunity to pause and *seriously* evaluate the way we talk about others, incite discrimination, contribute to systemic forms of injustice and the like. Reading today's *New York Times* cover story about the Norwegian suspect allegedly responsible for much of the cold-blooded carnage, including the calculated killing of children, I could not help but think of the horrendous remarks made by politicians and political aspirants in recent months. Particularly a handful of Republicans on the local and national level (not that there might not be Democrats, Libertarians, Independents, and others duly culpable, but I just don't know of any particular cases).

I think of one-time presidential hopeful Rep. Michele Bachmann (R-MN), particularly her and her husband's vocal and at-times vociferous and discriminatory attacks against LGBT people. According to a *Boston Herald* article: "[Marcus Bachmann is] the one who insists you can 'pray away the gay.' He's compared bisexuals and gays to 'barbarians' who must be "disciplined." Meanwhile, she has lamented that involvement in 'the gay and lesbian lifestyle' means 'personal bondage' linked to 'Satan.'"

I think of Rep. Peter King (R-NY) and his "crusade" against "Muslim Radicalism," made most visible in his call for Senator McCarthy-esque inquiry panels. He is recorded in the *LA Times* as saying: "'Today, we must be fully aware that homegrown radicalization is part of Al Qaeda's strategy to continue attacking the United States,' King said. 'Al Qaeda is actively targeting the American Muslim community for recruitment. Today's hearing will address this dangerous trend.'" His would-be "terrorist witch-hunt," openly discriminates against a population because of its religious tradition. Meanwhile some observers have noted with irony King's own support of the Christian terrorist group — the IRA — speaking publicly, such as in 1982 in a pro-IRA rally in New York, in favor of the group's behavior which was, as any sensible observer might note, religiously and politically motivated violence that was recognized the world over as terrorism.

I think of former Governor Sarah Palin and her repeated invocation of her now infamous phrase, "don't retreat, reload," proclaimed publicly as recently as July 12th of this year on the "Sean Hannity" program on the *Fox News Network*, long after commentators of all political persuasions called for reform in that sort of language after the Tucson shooting in January.

There are plenty more examples to share, but for the purpose of space, I will leave it to these three to illustrate my point for now. With this sort of public and political rhetoric, discrimination and behavior coming from women and men who have a national and international audience *and* proudly proclaim themselves Christian, one must seriously take pause in light of last week's events.

The *Times* reports that the Norwegian man charged with killing more than 90 people this week, "says he acted alone in a strike eerily foretold in a detailed manifesto calling for a Christian war to defend Europe against the threat of Muslim domination."

The worst act of terrorism in the relatively quiet Scandinavian country of Norway was caused by a radical Christian, not an "extremist Muslim." Who wants to kill whom? The report continues:

> The police identified the suspect as Anders Behring Breivik, 32, a right-wing fundamentalist Christian. Acquaintances described him as a gun-loving Norwegian obsessed with what he saw as the threats of multiculturalism and Muslim immigration.

What informs such a horrible action? I might suggest that, although one is always individually culpable for his or her actions, there are indeed those who contribute to an environment and discourse of violence that helps nurture the sick and evil seeds of hatred planted in the thoughts of such disturbed people. Why would anyone think that such horror could not take place on our soil?

If such an action did take place, not unlike the radical "Christians" that planned and executed the Oklahoma City attacks, who is there to blame? Homosexuals, Muslims, Immigrants? Or might we as a society be willing to look at our political leaders and their disgusting language and hateful discourse, the promotion of firearm ownership and "gun rights" by powerful groups like the NRA or the openly discriminatory homophobia, Islamaphobia and xenophobia that has become an expected feature of certain politicians' political platform?

The theoretical content of the Norwegian suspect's written material eerily jibes with much of what certain politicians and other conservative public figures have been saying in recent months and years: talk about implementing a "cultural conservative political agenda," a militarization of language, falsely equating Marxism with various social movements, just to name a few. The *Times* reports:

> In the 1,500-page manifesto, posted on the Web hours before the attacks, Mr. Breivik recorded a day-by-day diary of his months of planning. He said he was part of a small group that intended to "seize political and military control of Western European countries and implement a cultural conservative political agenda."
>
> He predicted a conflagration that would kill or injure more than a million people, adding: "The time for dialogue is over. We gave peace a chance. The time for armed resistance has come."
>
> The manifesto was signed Andrew Berwick, an Anglicized version of his name. A former American government official briefed on the case said investigators believed the manifesto was Mr. Breivik's work. Titled "2083: A European Declaration of Independence," it equates liberalism and multiculturalism with "cultural Marxism," which the document says is destroying European Christian civilization.

We need to change our discourse!

This sort of stuff has to end. Tolerance, acceptance, understanding, dialogue, and justice for all are the only ways we can promote peace in the world, in our nations and in our communities. The lesson for Norway for the United States is that *we* have to change. Let's work to make our world a more peaceable place before any other person or community has to suffer such tragedy.

Dear sisters and brothers in Norway, you are in our prayers.

July 24, 2011

68

The Sin of American Nationalism

"You shall not make for yourself an idol, whether in the form of anything that is in heaven above, or that is on the earth beneath, or that is in the water under the earth. You shall not bow down to them or worship them; for I the Lord you God am a jealous God, punishing children for the iniquity of parents, to the third and the fourth generation of those who reject me, but showing steadfast love to the thousandth generation of those who love me and keep my commandments" (Exodus 20:4).

This is the first of what I anticipate being a three-part installment on my reflections centering on the Independence Day of the United States, popularly recalled as the Fourth of July. This quote from Exodus, this listing of the First Commandment, is simply to set the tone for what is to come. It has been my increasing awareness and visceral experience of the symbols of an alternative state religion in the United States in recent years that leads me to reflect on this Hebraic passage today.

One has only to think about standing silently, hand over one's heart during the secular liturgy of a sporting event to conjure parallel images of rising to greet the processional cross as a presider reverences the Eucharistic Table. To what do we worship? To what do we bow down in homage?

The way many people talk about the United States bespeaks their true commitment of faith. I often hear people professing their Credo: "I would *die* for this country!" And, of course, the ones who usually die are the young and the poor, the minorities and the uneducated. Whereas "Christianity" is only paid lip service when sloppily invoked in false testimony to defend patriotic and jingoistic notions of the founding of a "Christian nation" that, ergo, should be intolerant of peaceful and centrist practitioners of other faiths who wish only to establish a place of worship and a community center in Lower Manhattan; To elicit but one example.

Few people are willing to *die* for their Christian faith. Of course I mean figuratively, for to suggest otherwise might imply my unintentional consent for those seeking martyrdom or some other form of solicited violence. What I mean, of course, is that in those areas of public discourse, political debate and popular parlance that meander into the realm of the religious or theologically relevant – here I mean stark *pro-life issues* like anti-capital punishment, the prohibition of torture, the end of warfare, the support of the poor and marginalized, healthcare for all, the defense of civil rights for all citizens regardless of race, gender, country of origin or sexual orientation – is precisely when one's Christian faith should come to the fore.

However, it is usually in attempts generously described as superficial that "Christianity" or the myth of a "Christian nation" are invoked in the public square, thereby de-legitimizing much of the force that comes with the authentic proclamation of the Gospel, the *kerygma* of Jesus Christ.

Time and again Jesus makes clear by His words and deeds that what is central to "carrying one's Cross and following him" is not the superficial and vapid dropping of His name in a political stump speech, but the concrete and prophetic efforts exercised in His name to bring justice, peace and love into the world. This is not done by lowering taxes at a time when the rise of the debt ceiling could be catastrophic for a nation toward which the rest of the world looks for pacing, nor is it done in the imperial expansion of military and political power in parts of the world whose exports benefit the "national interests" of the United States.

What does constitute authentic Christian discipleship today is when women and men work to fulfill the mission of Jesus Christ, which is, as Luke's Gospel reminds us: "To bring good news to the poor...proclaim release to the captives and recovery of sight to the blind, to let the oppressed go free, to proclaim the year of the Lord's favor" (Luke 4:18-19). What about the way our government has been operating in recent years "brings good news to the poor?"

And yet they stand with the hands over their hearts, professing the faith of the community in "One Nation Under God," while the good news is withheld from the poor, the captives remain detained, the blind still cannot see and the next generation fights a war for the rich over an ecologically destructive natural resource.

The sin of American nationalism is first and foremost a sin against the First Commandment. This implicates Christians and Jews alike. Meanwhile, the sin of American nationalism is also a violation of nearly every other commandment because it promotes the condition for the possibility of a whole slew of transgressions: murder, stealing (particularly from the poor), coveting (the systemic evil of modern capitalism) and so on.

While the events associated with July 4, 1776 are indeed historic and worth celebrating, let that celebration not be at the expense of a real examination of personal and societal conscience. As the fireworks light the sky and the parades fill our streets, may we find some time to recall who we really are and to whom our allegiance is really pledged! We are first and foremost citizens of Creation and the Human Family and our allegiance is to the God of Jesus Christ who has established a covenant with us that demands more than what we are usually willing to offer.

July 2, 2011

69

Does God Bless America? God Knows no Boundaries

As the 2012 Presidential campaign gets underway, early in the cycle though it may be, we hear a phrase that is common among politicians and public figures in the United States: "God Bless America!" Although most people utter these words unreflectively, or perhaps even sing them in the popular patriotic song of the same name, those three innocuous words, when put together, necessarily raise a troubling question for its hearers. The question has to do with one's image of God and one's image of country. Do those who close speeches and greet crowds or lead groups in song with these words believe that the United States (which is what I presume the word "America" means in this case, even though there are indeed dozens of American countries in both the Northern and Southern part of the Western Hemisphere) is special among the nations of the world? Does this uniqueness stem from Divine providence and selection? Whether a speaker believes these points or not, the hearer of the words might in fact conjure such images.

This is where I think it's important to reflect upon what it means for a nation and a people to be blessed by God. One thing it certainly *does not* mean is the "American Dream" notion of financial prosperity or the national-security hope of military dominance (such as was claimed against the "godless communists" of the Cold War) or social stability that comes with being a global imperial force. Yet, it is my hunch that most people who say "God bless America," reflexively mean just those things, among others.

If we look to Scripture we see the history of one particular nation, one group of people unfolding over time in their relationship with God the Creator. They are the ones who are called "the Chosen People," the ones favored by God. For in fact the blessing of Abraham includes the very foundation of what will become the Tribe of Israel some generations later. God is the one who indeed blesses that people, rescuing them from oppression as dramatized in the book of Exodus and journeying with them amid good times and bad.

Yet, history — ancient and modern — has revealed that the seeming "blessing" of God's chosen people has not resulted in those things implicitly desired in the "American" greeting (I hesitate to call something so flippantly tacked onto every public speech in a *pro forma* manner "a prayer"). The people of Israel, Scripture shows us, remained a minority population, a nation often persecuted, one with intermittent military strength, one that has endured and suffered some of the worst treatment of any group in history. Is this the blessing that US politicians seek for the United States?

No, I don't think so. Nor do I think such a simplistic rendering of salvation history in the experience of the people of Israel (a necessary abstraction for the purpose of this brief posting) suffices to illustrate the complexities of a people's relationship to its Creator.

What I am trying to do here is highlight the absurdity — and the blatant jingoism or even ethnocentrism, depending who says it — latent in the phrase "God bless America." For God does not bless one country over another, one (modern conception of) nation over and against others. Who God blesses are those who wholeheartedly enter into the covenant with God as Abraham, Jacob, Moses, and their descendants have. "You will be my people and I will be your God."

God has blessed the United States, but not in some quantitatively different sense from those in Somalia, for example. The disparity of wealth and of power in our world is not God's doing. The relative comfort, security and resources that so-called Americans have is not because God has "blessed" or "loved" the US any more than any other constructed government on the globe.

God does not know what an "America" is.

God knows no boundaries.

We create these constructs and draw the proverbial lines in the sand, separating peoples and accumulating resources: *we* do this, *God* doesn't. God loves all people: You and me and Osama bin Laden and George W. Bush and the Pope and the Dali Lama. The geographic distinctions we make are simply that, *our artificial distinctions.* Yet, we often act as though these things were divinely decreed and inherently sacred.

If you want to know how to "Bless America," or any other arbitrary collection of people, then heed the words of the prophet Micah. Blessings from God do not come in the form of wealth, power or war. Blessings come in the form of covenant with the Creator:

"What does the Lord require of you but to do justice, and to love kindness, and to walk humbly with your God?" (Micah 6:8)

DANIEL P. HORAN, OFM

August 17, 2011

PART 6

WASHINGTON THEOLOGICAL UNION
ANNUAL JAMES A. CORIDEN
VALEDICTORIAN ADDRESS (2012)

70.

Washington Theological Union
James A. Coriden Valedictorian Address (2012)[‡]

Thank you,

Dr. Brown.

Father Tillotson,

Sr. McLaughlin,

Father Greenfield and members of the Board of
Trustees, Faculty and Staff,

Family and Friends,

And the graduating class of 2012:

It is with great humility and gratitude that I stand here
before you this afternoon: as one among a host of Washington
Theological Union graduates that have had the great honor to
be educated, formed and inspired by this institution and its
faculty, staff and supporters. The WTU has irrevocably
shaped, for the better, the Church in the United States – and,
as we can see from the international diversity of the student
body over the years – the world.

To be given the privilege to address you on this most
celebratory day, while all-too-aware of the fading institutional
glow of the WTU's twilight, is no easy task. This task is made
more challenging by the recent events in these last years that
have seemed, at times, to damper the theological and
ministerial enthusiasm of those committed to service in the
Church and world, those such as the members of the
graduating class gathered here.

You are all too familiar with the misunderstanding that
has led to intervention in the work of theologians; the

[‡] Daniel P. Horan, OFM delivered these remarks, as the James A. Coriden
Valedictorian, on the occasion of his graduation from the Washington Theological
Union with his Master of Divinity degree, the same institution from which he
graduated two years earlier having earned a Master of Arts in Systematic Theology.
This was the last standard and public commencement exercise of the institution,
which announced its closure after more-than forty years of operation.

diminishing degree of trust the People of God has for its leaders in the wake of abuse crises and partisan political activism; the suspicion of those who advocate for justice and peace, reconciliation and ecumenism, instead of the repetition *of* and acquiescing *to* a narrower and more isolated agenda; the desire of some in leadership and elsewhere to inaugurate a so-called "leaner, smaller, purer Church," with seemingly little regard for the pastoral need and spiritual thirst of the Children of God; and, most recently, the confusing actions on the part of those concerned about women religious who have – lest we forget – dedicated their whole lives in service to the Church, which is the Body of Christ.

It is with all of these troubling 'signs of the time,' which reflect more the 'griefs and anxieties' than the 'joys and hopes' of the women and men of this age, that I reflected and prayed about what I might say today.

Two weeks ago, to the day, I sat in the Basilica of St. Mary of the Angels in the lower part of Assisi, Italy. I had been in Assisi for a gathering of theologians and ecumenists for a conference on peacemaking and interreligious dialogue. As the conference winded down, I snuck away early to pray at the little chapel that is the mother church and founding location for the Franciscan movement.

Called the *Portiuncula,* or "the little portion," this centuries-old chapel is about the size of one of our WTU classrooms. It is small and simple and was the church most loved by Francis of Assisi. In the centuries after his death, the Franciscans and the universal church, in order to honor and protect this sacred space, built a gigantic basilica over the *Portiuncula.*

The basilica church is simply huge, with an imposing presence outside in the open piazza and inside with its massive and overarching structure of marble and stone. My thought has always been that Francis was likely rolling in his grave at the thought of such opulence and excess. But then I realized something that might be insightful for us today. I asked myself: Where is *the Church* of St. Mary of the Angels? Is it this massive, imposing, stone basilica? Or is it the tiny, fragile, simple church, which is housed within?

The more I considered it, the more I realized that on the

one hand, it is both. They are intertwined, the large church protects and shelters the small church, it provides the context and sets the environment. Yet, the small church gives meaning and purpose to the large basilica and it is where Francis's heart was located. His work and his way of life arose out of the small church – the *little portion* – and transformed religious life and spirituality forever. If Francis were alive today, I wonder if he wouldn't still have problems with the big, imposing basilica; with its opulence and with the message it seems to project about what is important and what is not. But, Francis would likely not be as bothered as I can be at times today as a friar coming "home" to the spiritual center of my religious order. He would, I think, still focus his attention and energy and direct his love toward the little Church, the *Portiuncula*.

It is there that he came to hear the quiet voice of the Spirit calling him to live his baptismal vocation to the fullest.

It was there that the early brothers, inspired by the would-be saint, joined Francis in fraternity and ministry.

It was there that the young noblewoman Clare of Assisi professed her commitment to follow Francis's way of life.

It was there that women and men, the poor and the privileged, the powerful *and* the marginalized alike sought out the pastoral care and spiritual guidance of the man who would become Christianity's most popular saint.

It was there, at the *Portiuncula*, that Francis asked to have his naked body laid so that, as he entered this world in total poverty and completely dependent on God, he might leave this world in similar fashion.

And, I came to realize while praying in the tiny church, that all of us here have our own *Portiunculas*, our own "small portions" of the church, like Francis had St. Mary of the Angels.

For some of the graduates, your *Portiuncula* is at the side of a hospital bed or in the waiting room of an oncology wing, where your hearts are led by the Spirit to reveal the compassionate face of our loving God to the sick and dying.

For some of the graduates, your *Portiuncua* is found in the parish church where you help form the spiritual life of the faithful, minister to people during their most joyful and sorrowful moments, and share the good news of Jesus Christ in so many ways.

For some of the graduates, your *Portiuncula* is located in the classroom, educating students about the richness of the theological and spiritual traditions of our faith, guiding and mentoring the next generation of Catholics and other Christians during their most formative years.

For some of the graduates, your *Portiuncula* is in place yet to be imagined in a world that so desperately needs the Gospel, and with people who wholeheartedly long for the life-giving word that God loves them and journeys with them in life.

Like Francis of Assisi, each of us graduates has received – in some form or another – the vocational call of the Spirit to "Rebuild Christ's Church." When Francis famously received this call from the Lord at the chapel of San Damiano, it was not the large basilica, the massive overarching structures, or the immovable systems of old that he began to repair. No, brick-by-brick, stone-by-stone, person-by-person, Francis rebuilt, reinforced and cared for the "Little Portion," the *local* Church where his heart could be found.

In difficult times in the Church and world, our call as graduates of the Washington Theological Union is to "rebuild" the *Portiunculas* of our lives – those locations where ministry takes place and the encounter of Christ in one another is made manifest.

We have been *formed well* for the mission. We have received the best training one can conceive. We are the WTU's gift to the Church. And we have so many people to thank for that: the faculty, the staff, the administrators; our religious communities, our friends, our families: spouses, parents and children; and we have all those who have gone before us these 40+ years at WTU to thank as well.

In closing, I would like to share with you three theological themes that I believe might serve us well in our ministries and lives of faith. (It wouldn't be an academic exercise if I didn't include some seemingly esoteric theological reflection that, I hope – like our studies at WTU – turn into practical resources). They speak to me today and I hope they speak to you too... These themes are: (1) The Word, (2) The need for Piety, and (3) Jesus's last words from the Cross: "It is

Finished."

The first is the Hebrew term *dabar*, which means "the Word." But, as scholars of Hebrew Scripture know far better than I, *dabar* has another meaning or sense. It is both the Word as spoken *and* it means the action one takes. Remember that wherever we go, whatever we do, in our call to preach the "*Word* of God," we must preach with our actions as much as with what we say or write.

The second is the term *Piety*. I really believe that what the church needs is more piety in the lives of its ministers. I do not mean what "piety" has come to imply in recent years – an overtly devotional affect, for example. What I mean is what the word *piety* means at its root – from the Latin, *Pietas*. It refers to the duty, the responsibility, the relationship among family members. It is the care and concern that one owes a parent, a sibling, a child. Our Pious Action intrinsically means relationship with and our care for all of our sisters and brothers in Christ. So remember, that as we go forward in life, we should do so with piety, living our faith through loving action.

Finally, there is Christ's final words on the Cross: "It is Finished" as it appears in the 19th Chapter of John's Gospel. At first this seems like a sad end to a tragic story, but this is a matter of the fuller meaning being lost in translation. The Greek text is perhaps better translated as "it is *fulfilled*," meaning that what has begun in the life of the Lord – the in-breaking of the Kingdom of God – has been fulfilled, and now a new beginning is unfolding, the world will never be the same again. This is why we call graduation exercises a "commencement," because what at first seems like an end is, in fact, also a new beginning.

The closing of the Washington Theological Union after more than forty years appears to be a moment in which to cry out "it is finished!" But, another way to look at this moment is to recognize that the Spirit does not abandon our good works and that each ending is, like these commencement exercises, also a new beginning.

It will fall to each of us to carry forward into our lives and work all that has been passed on to us, recognizing that this day simultaneously marks a fulfillment *and* a start.

May each of us respond to Christ's call to "rebuild the church" in the little portions, the *Portiunculas*, of our ministry, using all of the tools, resources and formation we have received at WTU. May each of us preach *dabar* in word *and* deed; fulfill our ministry with *real* piety and recognize the new beginning that lies before us. And, finally, in the preferred greeting of St. Francis to all he met, I leave you with these words: *May the Lord give you peace!*

May 4, 2012

ABOUT THE AUTHOR

Daniel P. Horan, OFM is a Franciscan friar of Holy Name Province of the Order of Friars Minor (New York) and is currently a Ph.D. student in Systematic Theology at Boston College. He has previously taught in the Department of Religious Studies at Siena College and was a visiting professor in the Theology Department at St. Bonaventure University. He is the author of dozens of scholarly and popular articles in several journals and other periodicals, and of the books *Dating God: Live and Love in the Way of St. Francis* (Franciscan Media), *Francis of Assisi and the Future of Faith: Exploring Franciscan Spirituality and Theology in the Modern World* (Tau Publishing), and *Franciscan Priesthood: The Possibility of Franciscan Presbyters According to the Rule and Tradition* (Koinonia Press). You can read his blog at www.DatingGod.org. For more information and to learn more visit his website www.DanHoran.com

Praise for Daniel P. Horan, OFM's Earlier Books...

Dating God: Live and Love in the Way of St. Francis

"A fresh new voice in Christian spirituality who reminds us that the Creator is active in every moment of our lives and shows how our lives are filled with, as the Franciscans say, pax et bonum: peace and goodness."
– **James Martin, S.J.**, author, *The Jesuit Guide to (Almost) Everything.*

"Spirituality doesn't get any better than this! A splendid book!"
– **Michael Leach**, author, *Why Stay Catholic? Unexpected Answers to a Life-Changing Question*

"Dating God is the perfect primer on Franciscan spirituality"
– **Beth Knobbe**, author, *Party of One: Living Single with Faith, Purpose, and Passion*

Francis of Assisi and the Future of Faith: Exploring Franciscan Spirituality and Theology in the Modern World

"In Dan Horan's new book, we are introduced not to a decorative saint who got on well with birds but a man who shook the foundations of medieval Europe and who — along with other key figures of the early Franciscan movement — still challenges us today."
— **Jim Forest**, author, *All Is Grace: A Biography of Dorothy Day*

"As we celebrate the 50th anniversary of that great Council, Friar-Author Dan Horan opens the doors of the Church which for his generation is 'today,' not 'tomorrow!' Fr. Horan is particularly adept at translating the importance of a Franciscan approach for today's "digital natives." His voice is sure to capture the attention of contemporaries and create a bridge for older readers who know themselves to be strangers to this new way of learning and knowing."
— **Margaret Carney, OSF, STD**, president, St. Bonaventure University

"In a style that is both scholarly and highly readable, he brilliantly uncovers and elucidates the "foolish" wisdom of Franciscans as it is lived and voiced first of all in St. Francis and then as it is perpetuated and developed in significant Franciscan thinkers and saints from the Middle Ages to the present Millennial generation…The depth and range of this book makes it an indispensable source for how the Franciscan spiritual and intellectual tradition has been lived and voiced in the past and a blueprint for how it can be lived at the beginning of the 21st Century."

　　— **Murray Bodo, OFM**, author, *Francis: The Journey and the Dream*

"With a great spirit of prayer and devotion, Horan helps us discover how Francis of Assisi is anything but the patron of those who are spiritual but not religious, spiritual but not theological. Rather, Horan gives us sound spirituality and theology grounded in the perennially relevant and popular Franciscan tradition. Past speaks to the present and guides us into the future. Francis and Anthony both would be pleased."

　　— **Mary Stommes**, editor, *Give Us This Day: Daily Prayer for Today's Catholic*

CPSIA information can be obtained
at www.ICGtesting.com
Printed in the USA
BVHW041108270519
549332BV00024B/2203/P